Taking the Child's Way Home

ROB WILKINS

ZondervanPublishingHouse
Grand Rapids, Michigan

A Division of HarperCollins*Publishers*

Taking the Child's Way Home
Copyright © 1995 by Rob Wilkins

Requests for information should be addressed to:

▟ ZondervanPublishingHouse
Grand Rapids, Michigan 49530

Library of Congress Cataloging-in-Publication Data

Wilkins, Rob.
    Taking the child's way home / Rob Wilkins.
       p.   cm.
    ISBN 0-310-20019-9 (softcover)
    1. Christian life. 2. Wilkins, Rob. I. Title.
BV4501.2.W5325   1995
248.4—dc 20
                                         95–36280
                                            CIP

Edited by John Sloan and Rachel Boers
Interior design by Sue Koppenol

Printed in the United States of America

95 96 97 98 99 00 01 02 /❖ DH/ 10 9 8 7 6 5 4 3 2

To Tim, the captain of my childhood,
my brother in flesh and faith

Contents

Taking the Child's Way Home \ 9

1. Timelessness \ 25

2. Trust \ 43

3. Wonder \ 59

4. Fear \ 75

5. Innocence \ 91

6. Play \ 107

7. Imagination \ 125

8. Faith \ 141

9. Creativity \ 159

10. Love \ 177

Traveling Home \ 195

Taking
The Child's Way Home

*I tell you the truth, unless you change and
become like little children, you will never enter
the kingdom of heaven.*

MATTHEW 18:3 ✿

My car erupts in a cloud of steam along Illinois 58 just
past the forest reserve and just shy of the concrete edge of
suburbia. "Great," I spew forth, "on top of everything else,
now this!" My anger is fueled by disappointment, frustration, and deep loss. At the age of thirty-three, in the
prime of life, I am between jobs, burned out, as physically
sick as I have ever been, and longing for rest. "Lord," I
scream in silent frustration, "how did I get here?"

Bending down to look under the car, I see a stream of
fluid the yellow-green color of trouble. As I hit my head
against the bumper, I hear a small voice from the passenger side of the car. "Da-da." My two-year-old son, Taylor.
In my rage, I had all but forgotten. Instinctively, I lower
my voice, smile a weak smile, and begin muttering under
my breath like a cartoon character. Taylor giggles.

I know I must do something. The next gas station is
three miles down the road; the nearest house, if we follow

the road, is at least a mile away. And the stroller is at home. I remember a shortcut: If we cut through a field on our right, there is a house about three or four hundred yards back. I snatch Taylor from the car and we set off.

In my anger, I am focused on getting from here to there with the least amount of steps; after all, I have important things to do. But after just a few steps, my son begins chanting, "I wan da!" (translation: "I want down"). Determined to stay on a straight line, I continue forward, pounding my feet and my voice for emphasis. Taylor, equally focused, begins stating even more emphatically, "Da-da, I wan da!" In this Field of Nightmares, we are engaged in a contest of wills that I, dead tired of losing, have settled on winning.

Despite the tears and screams of my son, I continue onward. About halfway to my goal, Taylor pulls out the heavy artillery, the move that all parents of toddlers come to dread and respect. There is something about the human skeleton's transition between baby and child that allows a two-year-old's spine to turn into a Jell-O-like substance, allowing him to miraculously escape even the firmest of holds.

My car sending off SOS signals in the distance, I chase furiously after Taylor, who is wild with laughter. Even the sternest of reprimands can't break into his joy, cut short his gallop. It dawns on me that when it comes to this kind of fun, my son means business.

The scene repeats itself: I run after Taylor, catch him, pick him up firmly, and begin moving again from point A to point B; Taylor cries, works himself up to that certain point of frenzy, turns his back into Jell-O, escapes, and runs, zigzag, in the circle of his laughter. After three or four encores I am out of breath, out of will, and nearly out of my mind.

Overwhelmed with exhaustion, frustration, and an in-the-bone weariness of life, I sink to the ground. For the next ten minutes Taylor does somersaults, runs up the hill, down the hill, up the hill, down the hill, stops to carry on a conversation of gibberish with an ant or two, dances, falls, giggles, smells a flower, watches a jet paint on a bright blue spring canvas of a sky, and not even once thinks about what he is doing, what complete misery he is causing me.

Clearly, I think to myself, *Taylor has a lot to learn about priorities.* Here he is, running aimlessly back and forth in the middle of an abandoned field after scattered dandelion seeds, alternating between screaming at the top of his lungs and laughing so hard I think he will never catch his breath, while I alone know that getting home means making our way to the nearest phone.

But children often have a far different sense of direction. With Dad, a spring sky, a field of grass, and a few bugs, a child's way home is more the motions of trust, wonder, and faith, not in moving specifically east, south, north, or west. Home, in a child's mind, will just happen. It always does.

Although I try to hold on to my anger, my priorities, my desire to fix whatever is wrong, even I, deep into my broken, adult life, am not immune to the galloping giddiness of my son. Such a love of life is infectious. When he runs to the bottom of the hill, puts his head on the ground, and looks back through his legs at me, I crack a smile. After repeating this action fifty times or so, each one punctuated by an attack of the giggles, I start to laugh. Finally, I join him in his madness.

For all the passing world to see, we must seem out of our minds as we lose ourselves in ladybug finger dances, sloppy somersaults, dizzy circles of laughter, crooked lines of discovery, the random and chaotic movements of grace. A green crack in time, the unhurried budding of eternity, has occurred along Illinois 58.

Nearly two thousand years earlier, in a common town wedged in between thick, green vegetation and parched hillsides somewhere east of the Jordan River, Jesus is on his way out of Galilee and headed for Jerusalem, his final visit.

Even in this lonely country Jesus draws a crowd: the Pharisees, those religious experts intent on tripping him up; his disciples, who, even this close to the cross, have pathetic and serious misunderstandings about the kingdom of God; and the crowd, always the crowd, some seeking, some curious, some looking for who knows what.

Jesus is tired—not just in his feet from having walked so many miles, but in his soul. On the trip, a familiar fight had erupted among his disciples—who was to be the greatest in his coming kingdom? And this after he had told them of his coming suffering! Nothing seemed to be getting through. How many ways could he say it and still be misunderstood? The kingdom of God is a gift to receive, a realm to freely enter, not a thing to build or a vote to win.

And then, in the midst, come the children. Why have they been brought to Jesus? Was it a choice their parents made, like packing for a picnic, or was there something deeper drawing these little ones? In any case, they are here, dressed in their Saturday-go-to-Synagogue clothes—some still nursing on their mothers' breasts, some old enough to stand and walk, some jumping and calling and laughing the way children do. Those who can walk, run to him. Those who can talk, softly call out his name. Like the surge of rivers moving to the sea, their movement is natural.

The disciples, of course, attempt to keep the children from Jesus. Why? Maybe it is because they know Jesus is tired, bone weary, and he doesn't need to be bothered with drooling and jumping and simple questions. Maybe they feel Jesus needs a lesson or two in efficiency, given his earlier failures to capitalize on critical opportunities. Or maybe they think that, in the scheme of things, children aren't worthy of Jesus' time. If Jesus sees these children, the word will certainly get out—"bring your children to see Jesus"—and then what kind of shape will the world be in?

For whatever reason, when Jesus hears that the disciples have rebuked those who brought the children to see him he is indignant, troubled in spirit to the point of pain. He pleads with his disciples for understanding. "Let the little children come to me. Do not hinder them," he says.

As the children come, Jesus invites as many as will fit to sit in his lap. He hugs one, perhaps a six-year-old girl with buckteeth, looks at his disciples, smiles, and says, "I tell you the truth, anyone who will not receive the kingdom of God like a little child will never enter it." And then, from somewhere within the depths of Jesus, is it the disciples' imagination or do they hear him laugh—a sound as pure as the blue of the sky?

As the disciples watch, they see little children who have been brought for just one touch being smothered with the love of God. Little children, incapable of argument or politics or persuasion, freely experiencing the person of God. Little children, with diapers or humility or skinned knees, fully receiving the gift of a lifetime. The disciples see the love of Jesus, unbroken by human pride and open to any possibility, flowing freely to the children. Not only does he touch and bless, he hugs each child tenderly and fervently, time and time again.

The kingdom has come—with love and familiarity, with great power and authority. Do the disciples see this?

Four years later, I still look back on the choice I made in that field as a turning point of my life. I could either drive myself deeper into adult despair or begin the process of rediscovering child-like wonder.

The decision was not so much one of whether or not to play with my son, but of adopting an entirely different perspective of life. In the years following my first awareness of salvation, a curious thing had been happening—my faith, like the slow leaking of a balloon, was losing its buoyancy. It should have been just the opposite. I was, from nearly every angle, taking the necessary steps to make sure my faith was rising—praying, discipling, serving, fasting, teaching, using my spiritual gifts, taking seriously the commands of my Lord—yet I was sinking in a growing despair. The more I tried to do to get myself out of the situation, the more weary I felt. When I had the time, I would search and search for where my spiritual air was leaking out, but I could find no visible errors in methodology. Whatever it was, I could not fix it with a patch.

And then, in that field, it first hit me. The problem was that, in my carefully measured steps of faith, I had wandered from the grace that had first humbled and empowered me. Instead of seeing life and salvation as a gift beyond comprehension, I had begun, subtly and over a long period of time, to see faith as my level-headed duty. Obedience, settled in an unstirred love, became my focus. I knew for a fact that the world was a serious place that required from me some serious business. I saw time ticking in the light of eternity. "Be very careful, then, how you live—not as unwise but as wise, making the most of every opportunity, because the days are evil" (Ephesians 5:16). Lost people were headed for hell. The church, the very body of Christ, needed to be grown and strengthened. A spiritual battle of unthinkable proportions raged around me. There was no time to waste on simply being, or even being still: the God of the cosmos was depending upon me.

But, more and more, all of this action was stripping away the one thing that could sustain and empower: the environment of grace. In that abandoned field, I became aware once again of the wild movement of grace in my two-year-old. Taylor did not observe, like a man taking notes, but was overcome with what he saw. He did not act with careful and studied precision but abandoned himself in laughter, somersault, and the dizzy spinning of the world. Fully occupied with life and grace, he simply responded—with energy, with unconscious worship, with galloping joy, with openness and humility and unbounded expectations.

The Bible tells us that our faith should be just as child-like. The good news is not just a one-time proclamation, but the unceasing eruption of God for us, with us, and in us. Our spring field is the assurance of the unending bloom of life and grace.

Please do not misunderstand. This book is not about escaping from Christian responsibility, duty, obedience, or hard work. We live in a broken, fallen, pain-filled world desperately in need of the wild surprise of redemption. We are sinners, each and every one of us, so naturally drawn toward sin and doubt that we must practice a life of obedience and discipline. We must not become like little children by *doing* what they do—dancing and leaping aimlessly in abandoned fields. At least, not most of the time. Yet, in ways critical to our faith, we must *be* like little children. After all, little children—with nothing to offer, nothing to bargain with, helpless, dependent, trusting, open to any possibility—are the ones blessed with grace who God can move.

If we are to learn from children—and Jesus said that we should—then we must re-enter the realm of childhood. But before we do so, we must get a perspective of its potential dangers and rewards. There are two equal and opposite errors that we, as adults, can make about the realm of childhood. The first, and most obvious, is to choose never to leave it, preferring the weightlessness of self to the gravity of the world. The second is to leave it altogether, exchanging the wildness of wonder for the mathematics of rules. The way each of us chooses to relate to childhood deeply influences the way we live.

For those who choose never to grow up, life is a series of disconnected events centered in self, loosed of authority, that seeks only to seize the day, playing the odds in any given moment for a payoff of happiness. Potential is always being birthed; yet, without any sort of discipline, it often becomes chaos.

Those who completely discard childhood strip themselves of the essentially child-like qualities of trust, imagination, and humility. They are left with mostly adult tools—the hammer of logic, the nails of words, the unforgiving fire of dreams. These people feel so strongly about discipline and control that they don't allow *any* chaos into their lives.

Society, as well, is split between these two approaches to life. One approach is carefree and individualistic, bound by only the fulfillment of one's own desires. Such are the promiscuous, the actors, the alcoholics, the party animals, those who invite you to dance in the streets. For this part of society, responsibility is the antonym of fun. Their behavior is childish.

Society's other approach is that of the morally or religiously earnest. The adults in this segment of society are bound to do good or, failing that, at least follow the rules. From their perspective, everything depends upon their correct words and actions. Because their opinions are at once impossibly narrow and bloated, they must rely on change to occur through coercion, not persuasion. Mostly, they wonder why they don't get any respect. Such are the politicians, the do-gooders, the philosophers, the religion hawkers—all those who work as hard as is humanly possible for something better. For these people, fun is useful only if it restores them to the cause. Their behavior is churlish.

These two attitudes in society are not new. In that lonely town somewhere to the east of the Jordan River, Jesus was addressing both the churlish and the childish when he said, "I tell you the truth, anyone who will not receive the kingdom like a little child will never enter it."

To the Pharisees, champions of the churlish, the message was this: only a child is wise enough to know she can't wrap the arms of God around her. Jesus was trying to make these so-called experts of the law understand that all human effort, no matter how pious or sincere or noble-looking, is destined to degenerate into rules, the kind of decomposition that you find in sin, in death, in the ashes of a tomb.

For the disciples, Jesus' message made a distinction between their adult childishness and what it means to be a child of God. They needed to be child-like in attitude: helpless, humble, open. Unless they understood that the kingdom is received as a gift and not taken by wrestling, all their petty positionings would get them exactly where they would least like to be—out of the kingdom altogether.

Together, the Pharisees and disciples shared the root misunderstanding that, in one way or another, their standing in the kingdom was up to them. Jesus, on the way to the cross, was about to fully reveal to them another quite dramatic option, the one most rooted in a child-like perspective: death and resurrection. Eugene Peterson, in his book *Traveling Light*, says:

> If we are going to live freely in and for and with God, neither being good nor having fun counts for anything, but only a new creation; not keeping rules or breaking rules, but a new creation; not reviving the old-time religion or swinging with the new pagans, but a new creation; not circumcision or uncircumcision, but a new creation; not what you do, but what God does; not what I do, but what God does.

This is the truth, Jesus says, that is hidden from the proud and revealed unto little children and to all those who are truly child-like.

I have often wondered—what is it exactly about little children that Jesus finds so attractive? Just today, my four-year-old son managed to crack his brother's skull with a plastic Tyrannosaur, spill a cherry-red Mondo on an expensive tapestry rug, whine about having the wrong cup, and cry over a dead ladybug. When I seek to understand what Jesus meant when he said to become like children, I am fully convinced of what he *didn't mean.*

Clearly, God wants us to mature—to move from self-centered behavior to God-centered love. Ephesians 4:15 states, "Speaking the truth in love, we will in all things grow up into him who is the Head, that is, Christ." But at the heart of Jesus' words, as is most often the case, is the paradox that to be fully mature, we must remain childlike. Part of the solution to that puzzle, I believe, is in those marvelous qualities this book is structured around: trust, wonder, imagination, dependence ... but even these are just symptomatic of a deeper kind of characteristic peculiar to childhood: that of experiencing life as a gift.

Ignorant of time, distance, and measurement, a child is open and vulnerable to the world. In every sense out of control, he lives by dependence and trust; is ambushed, moment after moment, by wonder, fear, and surprise; breathes and moves by imagination, faith, and play. In other words, life is something that *happens* to a child, not something of his own creation.

In a fundamental sense, then, a child is humble. She has no illusions about the monarch butterfly that she chases, the feel of a cotton blanket in her sleep, the dog that howls into the night, the pink stroke of a mother's hand. They are simply and suddenly there or not there. This dependence, this trust, is the beginning of faith, the beginning of maturity. It is what God wants from his children.

In the slow and often unnoticeable movement from child to adult, it is possible to lose as much as we gain. As we learn to control and manipulate our worlds instead of being spun by the magnitude of each moment, we move toward independence, skill, and purpose. But the danger in our efforts to work, create, and secure a living—to become fully mature adults—is that, without knowing it, we begin to believe that what we *do* is more important than who we are or what we have been given. Control, because it is ultimately an illusion, requires more and more of us. If I could secure this promotion, my child's future would be solid. If I could acquire this car, my image would be solidified. If I could coach little league, my ministry could expand. If I could stay on this diet, I could finally earn respect. The illusion of control always demands at least one more thing to do.

Technology, the ultimate tool in building illusions, gives us the ability to shorten the time required to do everything. Seconds, even milliseconds, become critical, with the underlying assumption that if we could just do more, we would get what we wanted or needed. Efficiency is the answer. The problem is, we have become so occupied with doing more—processing information, enrolling in enrichment classes, making meals for the sick—that we have worked ourselves into a frenzy and no longer have the time or energy to remember what we started out to accomplish in the first place. We become numb, which is often mistaken for a blessing. A day becomes just another day; an unbeliever, a salvation project; a fresh snow, an annoyance; and God, just someone who is somewhere *out there*. We are devoid of imagination. By giving ourselves over to the cultural god of efficiency we run the risk of losing those child-like qualities that should frame the core of who we are—our capacities for surprise, dependence, simple trust.

In between childhood and adulthood, in the splintering movement from dependence to control, the world often gets warped. Work gets confused with value, results with strategies, numbers with purpose, busyness with importance. Soon we become anxious adults, not laughing children: doing, not being; talking, not singing; acting, not responding; existing, not experiencing. We allow very little time for God, his gifts, his promises, his love.

Let me take you back to that abandoned field once more. The difference between adult despair and child-like wonder is this: little Taylor blowing dandelion seeds in the wind. In his mind, the dandelion is not just another weed in a weed-weary world, but a singularly significant event, perhaps the most astonishing achievement in the known history of the world for, by some kind of magic, the seeds fly. "Dada—ooook!" he cries, and he means, with his child-like intensity, to *really* look. To see these windborn seeds as *he* is seeing them—with wonder, amazement, respect, and a wordless kind of breathlessness. There they are, these dandelion seeds, leaping in the wind, catching sun in silk, dancing orange spark, their symmetry of line and angle precise and endless, poised for a chance breeze. Half a mile and a phone call away from home, I lie on my back and look, really look, at these wild and common seeds, dancing with such grace, full of all the power of life.

Finally, slowly, I begin to see, in just such one impossible seed, a dancing and spacious grace: God with us, God for us, God living in us, and, only then, God working through us.

1 TIMELESSNESS

Take a commonplace, clean it and polish it, light it so that it produces the same effect of youth and freshness and originality and spontaneity as it did originally, and you have done a poet's job.

JEAN COCTEAU ❦

What I remember of childhood are mostly moments, both fleeting and eternal. A 1957 red Ford Falcon station wagon, the night settling in a purple cream sky. The whisper of my father in the falling dark is only half heard: "I love you, little one." I stir, feel his arms slide around my five-year-old body, feel the stubble of his cheek, the callous of his hand, his strong and familiar scent.

We move. In his arms I stir, skim the surface of consciousness, catch pieces of reality—slow echoes of a dog's bark, a yellow porch light, the bandy of moths, a sandpaper whisper, "We're home."

Through the screen door with its unoiled squeak of welcome, up the stairs, through the hall, and I am by my bed, still on my father's shoulder. Outside, yellow heat lightning flickers in the distance like the wordless jangling of nerves. The silence wraps around us. We slip along the edge of reality, our breathing as one, locked in the rhythm of safety. And then I am asleep, deep in the night, dreaming in vivid color.

Or the end of another evening, the end of another summer. The cicadas are winding down, and there is a hint of fall in the purple light at dusk. In the backyard, my parents are throwing a party. The shadows from the campfire dance wildly on the bark of trees, angle themselves onto the side of the garage, and spill into the cracked cement sidewalk.

I am apart from the other children, simply too young to break the secret code of whatever game they are playing. Then I hear it: my mother's laugh. Even though I cannot see her, I know by its architecture that it is hers. Her laugh could always find its way to my ears. My sadness at being left out is thrown into the company of my mother's joy. Sitting there in the twilight, I become aware of other sounds as if in a dream: voices slow and thick, dissolving one on top of the other; the bark of a dog; a train in the distance. What is this feeling running along my spine? As my mother's laugh fades, I am left dazzled by the beauty in the world.

My childhood home stands as a timeless memory in my mind: a two-story black and white farmhouse with a front porch, living room fireplace, an upstairs bathroom, kitchen, den, dining room, and three bedrooms. Most of the floors were wooden, so that if you put a good ear to the upstairs hallway, you could hear the buzzing of bees in the north wall.

The house sat on a couple acres of land situated near the small town of Van Buren. Van Buren, true to its name, was unspectacular, cautious, but not without a certain timid appeal: it consisted of a narrow, two-story grocery store; a fire station that served donuts and cider at Halloween; Ed's Bar and Grill, which was, as near as I could figure, owned by a woman named Pearl; and another store that sold anything from antiques to trailer parts to sewing needles. Two miles or so east of town stood Van Buren State Park, which held a dam, lots of muddy water, and, years later, a restaurant that played a good deal of country and western music.

But the town was of little concern to us. We were in the country, with only one immediate neighbor caddy-corner to the southwest and a more distant, not to mention more mysterious, neighbor a half mile north on Old Dixie Highway, shrouded in tall grass and drawn shades. That was it. Dad, Mom, Bev, Jim, Tim, and I were, for the most part, abandoned to ourselves.

There was, I must confess, very little excitement where we lived, as that word is generally understood. My father worked on the railroad; my mother was a housewife who later took on a part-time job at Britt's department store. When I was in fifth grade, the Van Buren Black Knights, directed by my brother Jim at point guard, made it to the Class A regional finals. My sister had made the cheerleading squad a couple of years earlier, and drove us buggy with such graceful poetry as "Rebound-a-bound-bound-

bound-rebound." Our dog, after a gland operation in his behind, had to wear diapers. And my brother Tim, who was just one year older than me, constantly astonished us with new and creative ways to split his head open.

But that was about it. Well, maybe it wasn't; maybe there were a dozen secret disasters, but that was all that we, as children, knew about. Our parents worked hard to create a safe world for us. When I look back on childhood, there is, first and foremost, a feeling of being embraced—not just in the arms of our parents, which we certainly and often were—but by a larger reality, an invisible, unspoken force. It was as if our world was bubbled, shielded, private—almost like living inside a terrarium. We needed nothing and had little to fear.

These memories are the skeleton, if you will, of my childhood. Each child, of course, has such memories: without love, a cage of bones; with love, the flesh and muscle of freedom. Timeless, in either case.

How can we speak of the *time* of childhood when a child knows so little of time? Try explaining *tomorrow* to a four-year-old or *month* to a child plastered all over today and there is only ignorance. In the rising of consciousness, children are only vaguely aware of the passing of time, in much the same way that a skier is aware of snow. Children simply go with the flow.

Even as I am writing this paragraph, I am observing my son Ethan from my study window. As I have been watching, he has built a road in his sandbox, chased a butterfly that fluttered into his view, played with a toy racing car that he stepped on, cried when one of its wheels stuck, and, after the tears dried up, chased his little brother with a garden hose. He is now a fountain of giggles. What is the flow of time to him?

Why is it that when I think back on my own childhood I remember only fragments, the small and common things: sparks on my father's grindstone, the slimy coupling of nightcrawlers under a flashlight, a one-armed Gumby? These come to mind attached to no particular order or time, powerfully fused into deep parts of me like a cotton candy spin, a sticky pale pink weave of unconnected moments, people, events.

As an answer to why memories don't form in a linear fashion, a neurophysiologist might suggest that children have an incomplete and evolving system of synapses. A sociologist would probably hint at an undeveloped sense of relational skills. But I suspect it goes deeper than that. I think adults often have a difficult time remembering and describing our childhoods because we have become anchored in time. We arrange words, thoughts, even life in a linear direction from beginning to end, here to there, left to right. A child's world is not so ordered.

Childhood, I believe, is the one and only point in life when we are free of time, when we are brave enough, safe enough, and foolish enough to experience life as it comes in its manic and wonderful spread of color, smell, decay, texture, splash, and sprout. Because a child has not yet been inoculated with the concepts of time, space, and order, he is left to be blasted with life.

Is it any wonder, then, that children look so dazed or silly or wide-eyed? Life is happening all around them, all at once. Who knows what the world could break into at any moment with the flick of a wrist, the break of a day, the beat of a heart?

Bombarded so, children respond with wildness, a bewildered, passionate energy. They gallop, sing, cry, scream, and giggle as if their very lives depended upon it. We disarmed adults would think and maybe even say "It's not that big of a deal," but children know no better. For them, life simply explodes. There is no let up, not really ever—even in their dreams there are sparks and teeth and primary colors. With only their babbling, ticklish wits to protect them, they are laid bare, flesh and bone and soul, to the movement of life in all its fullness. For them, each moment is a gift.

Children liked Jesus. In a way, this surprises me. Perhaps I have known too many leaders, sharp and coiled, waiting to strike, to hone, to focus, to do their best. They always say they are making the most of their time. Children do not like them; they see them, I think, as slightly out of kilter, like a bee with one wing or a laugh that tries too hard.

Scriptures, in fact, paint an often somber and stoic picture of Jesus. We don't know, for sure, that he laughed. Only twice do we know that he cried. At least once, he was angry. Given such an absence of information, it is easy to picture the face of Jesus as either pinched in the purpose of the cross or divinely blank, like he was always on some other higher yellow-gold realm.

Yet children loved to be near Jesus. Why was Jesus, this leader of leaders, different? Did he pull a denarius out of little Levi's ear? Did he blow bubbles? Did he set aside time, maybe an hour after synagogue, to play jacks, jump rope, or sail a boat of twigs? Or did children, by instinct, sense a camaraderie with Jesus? For here was a person—an adult, no less—who, like them, was unfettered, unshaken by the movement of time.

Unlike most adults, Jesus did not attempt to arrange, control, or neuter life through time. Instead, like a child, he fully experienced each moment, facing life with a kind of recklessness that was interpreted as full-hearted and foolhardy. Remarkably, he made no plans, no defenses, no appointments. He often scared adults, especially those crafted in control—shook them, like marbles in a glass jar, with the steady and wild insistence that abundant life was not what they thought it was.

Jesus knew that the only true control in life was in surrendering to the Father's will. Given over completely to the will of God—to love God and love others—he was remarkably and completely free of manipulation, defensiveness, apathy, and bitterness. Freed from the idea that he had to make life *work*, he lived a life of wonder, trust, imagination, dependence and vulnerability.

Time was not a thing to bleed for all it was worth, but to be experienced.

In much the same way as a child, Jesus seemed to live somewhere other than in the long shadow of time. When you read the Gospels, there isn't the feeling that Jesus had much of a long-range plan outside of the cross, but that he simply found it enough to move—hearing, feeling, healing, forgiving, crying, grieving, cleansing, laughing—in a world of pain, beauty, death, joy, and fear.

As I read and reread the Gospels, I am increasingly struck, not with Jesus' power, his doctrine, or the sureness of his hand or mind, but with the way he laid himself open, unprotected, dangerously and almost insanely moving to the razor-edge of harm. The man seemed to have no defenses. He told the truth until it killed him. He let the crowds swallow him. He allowed his soul to ache in sorrow and compassion. He marveled at unbelief, faith, and the enormous springing power in the smallest of seeds. He raged against religion, death, the eternal ash of sin. He fought against stubborn pride and hard hearts and beat his head on concrete realities. He partied like a winebibber. He loved sinners, drank with them, ate with them, shared stories with them, joked with them, and, finally, swallowed their sin. He spoke of wonderful and mysterious things. He prayed like he meant it. He slept in deep sleep. He slipped into solitude the way a night falls in the desert. He harmed no one, healed many, and loved his friends. He died naked, bleeding, and alone, crying into the deepest night the world has known.

There was, in Jesus, something lurking, stirring, laughing, trembling, as necessary as oxygen, as fierce as fire that leaped in his eye. It caught the children in-between breaths. It stunned them, left them gasping in laughter and frozen in sticky joy. "Time does not tick; it reveals," he seemed to be telling them. And that is, I believe, why the children came.

In my childhood home, the stairway was bulky and darkly stained, and, over time, its edges had been worn smooth and pale.

I don't know why, decades later, that staircase sticks in my mind. Maybe because it was the first thing you saw when you opened the front door, maybe because of the subconscious connections—up and down, day and night, living and sleeping. I suspect it is because, here, in this world of in-between, that I remember so often being struck, dazzled. It was there that I woke up on a high step, awakened literally to the fact that I was alive, and cried for my mom. In winter, I felt the break of cold on my skin as I raced down the stairs, fighting for the nearest register below. In the summer, there was a breeze there, a soft whisper like a dove's, stirring something inside me.

There were, too, the accidents: the preschool movements that could not make the distance to the upstairs bathroom. The early morning Christmas wanderings, simply out of our minds with anticipation, bending over the stairway railing to see what we should not yet see. The crayoned pictures on its long, angled wall.

And the transitions. My sister, Beverle, red-headed and teenaged, stomping up the stairs to her bedroom as though there was a bass drum under each of her feet, and my dad, following in the wake of such a beating, saying, "Don't you slam that door, young lady. Don't you slam that door," which, of course, she always did. Or our Boston terrier, Tuffer, watching with terror in his eyes, as my brother Tim and I tested the potential safety of a ride down the steps in a cardboard box. Or another school morning, just about any morning, down the stairs to the routine of chatter and breakfast and good-bye hugs, the warm scattering of dreams.

And the intrigue. During late-night parties, seduced by the strong smell of coffee and careful laughter of adults, the stairs acted as spy center, launch pad, escape route; *Your mission, should you decide to take it* was to make it underneath the dining room table, not giggle, and return undetected.

The staircase was solid and central in many ways: the progression of its steps, one after the other; the pre-dictability of law—up follows down follows up follows down; the certainty of monotony and thrill of another morning, another night. In the waking and sleeping worlds separated by those stairs, life was something that happened to us, and very seldom was it something of our own making. Like the incarnate Jesus, we each experienced the full blast of life in all of its wildness and strangeness and beauty, unanchored and unprotected by the precise ticking certainty of time. That stairway was, in one sense, the closest thing we had to time in that it alone served as a way for us children to mark the movement in our lives.

For, after all, how can we measure the movement from the world of a child to the world of an adult? Is it simply a progression of years, the distance between the place you live now and the place you lived then? Twenty-five or forty or fifty years and, say, two hundred miles?

These kind of measurements, one dimensional as they are, will never get at the question, for the greatest distance between a child and an adult is a change of perspective. What we are talking about is not simply something that moves in one direction, changing only points on a line, but a complete makeover of the world, like the pumping up of a folded beachball. When you see things differently, little remains the same.

We move, of course, from chaos to control, from spontaneity and recklessness to discipline and logic. From the newborn in the crib—bewildered, almost overwhelmed by color, light, shadow, and form—to the thirty-seven-year-old man with precision creases in his suit, buried in the *Wall Street Journal*. It is a change that occurs not so much *over* time, but *under* time. In fact, once time has been recognized, the changes are almost complete. A Mickey Mouse watch, once completely understood, becomes the beginning of the end of childhood.

At first there are the silly, two-tons-on-the-tongue syllables of *dada, mama, papa, pee-pee, bye-bye*—elemental words with names as bulky as lumps of clay to train the tongue, the teeth, the diaphragm. Toys are accompanied by bells, flashes, or jumpy brash surprises to train the eyes, hands, and synapses. And finally, at school, we learn math, spelling, reading, history, and penmanship.

All of this, of course, is for the purpose of *doing* something. Instead of merely reacting to the world in play or wonder or fear, we learn to pick up a toy, to swing a bat, to climb a ladder, to sound out a word, to hammer a nail, to swat a fly, to focus a thought—to move into life with purpose and control. With tools and strategies, we build houses, write books, run nursing homes, grow vegetables, teach in church, raise our children, take care of other responsibilities. Through the adult characteristics of perseverance, reason, and work, we carefully construct what each of our worlds is to be, or, at the very least, what they might become.

For the most part, this movement from infant to adult is good and necessary, as unstoppable and vital as the movement of the sun from east to west. An adult, through the careful application of time, space, and distance, will become competent, responsible, and careful and will find or create his or her place in the world. If this movement from child to adult did not happen and we were all left to the mercy of our uneducated wits, who would build our houses, fight our diseases, carve our pies, or change our diapers? God knows, there is much to be done. Who can question the benefits of reason, logic, calculation, past, present, future—those linear, left to right movements of life?

The problem with control is that, like all good things, it can get taken to an extreme. With all the tools at our disposal, we begin to fall into a mistaken impression that we are responsible for making our world spin, for creating our own happiness, security, fulfillment, and progress. We are tempted to use the tool of control to take care of ourselves first. A picket fence becomes a wall; a broken heart becomes a fortress; a God-given gift becomes a "ticket to the top." We get busy, addicted, panicky. Our energy is consumed with pursuing pleasure and escaping pain. Disconnected from who we are—children of God—these self-directed efforts often result in numbness and greed. In such a life there is little left for us but to grow old.

Those of us locked in this world of time know how difficult it can be to escape its boundaries. Time is larger than life in our culture—almost everything works against spontaneity. We have day-timers and stop-watches in our offices; home calendars hold class times and doctor appointments and school plays. We have been trained to be diligent workers and consumers—perfunctorily doing some thing at some time—and, in our nearly unconscious *doing*, have interrupted the pulse and rhythm of life. Even our *free* time consists of scheduling dates, managing projects, and setting goals. I know of one devoted Christian who has gotten so busy he has been reduced to scheduling his spontaneous moments for Thursday mornings!

There is, however, a problem with this kind of thinking. More often than not, the management of time often ends up becoming the hoarding of time. I love what Frederick Buechner writes about this idea:

> There are lots of people who get into the habit of thinking of their time as not so much an end in itself, a time to be lived and loved and filled full for its own sake, but more as just a way-station on the road to somewhere else, to a better job or the next vacation or whatever.

Remarkably, there is never the feeling that Jesus was pushed by time. He had time enough to be alone. Time enough to pray. Time enough to listen to little children. Time enough to save the world.

This is not to say that we should be unconcerned about time management. Ephesians 5:15–16 says that we should "be very careful, then, how you live—not as unwise but as wise, making the most of every opportunity, because the days are evil." Clearly, the Bible does not advocate a lazy existence, but asks us with diligence and discipline to work and suffer for the kingdom of God. Jesus accomplished everything *he* needed to accomplish.

The same sense of timelessness that surrounded Jesus is critical for our development as God's children. Viola Spolin, a theater director, urges:

> Through spontaneity we are re-formed into ourselves. It creates an explosion that for a moment frees us from handed-down frames of reference, memory choked with old facts and information and undigested theories and techniques of other people's findings. Spontaneity is the moment of personal freedom when we are faced with reality, and see it,

explore it and act accordingly . . . It is the time of discovery, of experiencing, of creative expression.

This sense of free and creative spontaneity is central to the world of the child. In fact, it is so central that all of the other attractive characteristics of children—those I will write about in later chapters—flow, directly or indirectly, out of it.

What, then, must we do to regain a more child-like perspective on time, and yet remain responsible adults in the real world of business, relationships, and daily living? We must be careful here, for the question itself is faulty, and reveals an adult preoccupation with time. "What must I do to become more child-like?" Once we have asked the question, the possibility for the change desired is lost. It is like asking for another To-Do list, this one designed to get us out from underneath all of our other To-Do lists.

Instead, we must cultivate the child-like perspective of Jesus. While purposeful and focused, he continued to experience life, moment by moment, in all its fullness.

As we seek to apply Jesus' attitude about time into our lives, we should be asking ourselves tough questions as to our underlying beliefs. These might include:

- How much of your time is spent on doing things to make *life work*? How many of the things you are working for have already been promised to you by God? If most of us look closely, we will see that a good deal of our time is spent accomplishing what has already been accomplished for us.

- How much of your time is spent in open, heart-to-heart relationships? For Jesus, relationships were at the heart of his time.
- Of the goals you wish to achieve, how many of them are buried sometime in the future? If time is something that you are consistently hoarding with the idea of a better life somewhere down the road, this should serve as a warning sign.
- Does your *doing* flow out of *being?* In order to gain a more child-like perspective about time, we must not simply ask how we can *do* more, but how we can *be* better. If we experience time to simply *be*—to hear and surrender to the wild and living voice of God, to open the heart and be shaped by grace, to stand in awe of a sunset or a blood-red cross—then the time when we must *do* will not be spent from an exhausted and bankrupt soul.

If we answer these questions honestly, stripping ourselves of selfish demands of time, we will find what is the child-like wisdom of Ecclesiastes 3:

There is a time for everything, and a season for every activity under heaven: a time to be born and a time to die, a time to plant and a time to uproot, a time to kill and a time to heal, a time to tear down and a time to build, a time to weep and a time to laugh, a time to mourn and a time to dance, a time to scatter stones and a time to gather them, a time to embrace and a time to refrain, a time to search and a time to give up, a time to keep and a time to throw away, a time to tear and a time to mend, a time to be silent and a time to speak, a time to love and a time to hate, a time for war and a time for peace.

Such words are poetry. In life there is rhythm. When we open ourselves to the timeless movement of God and the beauty and grace surrounding us, we are, in a real sense, spontaneously born again and again.

2 TRUST

It is impossible to go through life without trust: that is to be imprisoned in the worst cell of all, oneself.

GRAHAM GREENE ❧

I have always sensed order in my father and, from that order, power. Even in appearance, my dad seemed to exude a careful symmetry and balance: nearly every body part, almost as if by force of will, was held in taut and careful proportion.

As I look back through boxes of black-and-white photographs, I now realize that my father was not a large man. This always comes as a surprise to me, for his coiled muscles, bristled face, and the spark in his eyes all made him seem larger than life. There is a picture of him with my brother Tim and me at the edge of the Grand Canyon. Maybe it is the low fog or the angle of the picture, but, to this day, my father does not seem to be swallowed by the immensity of the surroundings. He stands firm, smiling, his arms around us, unfazed by the fierce yawn of earth just a foot or two away.

There was nothing particularly striking about my father, at least when taking an inventory of his individual features. He had slightly larger than normal ears balanced by a slightly larger than normal nose, combed back hair, straight and white teeth, a strong smile. Yet the overall effect was somehow greater than its parts; between his propensity for both intensity and silliness, he exuded a certain tension, charisma.

His arms were the only part of my father that broke with his otherwise careful proportion—they were as long as a gorilla's and seemed to sprout from his sleeves. But even though we used to joke with him about them, we always loved my father for his arms—for, time and again, they were the arms that provided for, healed, and protected us.

I remember one incident especially when my father's arms came to the rescue. It was a summer afternoon, and my two brothers and I were climbing trees in our backyard. Tim, who was maybe six at the time, had chosen a good sturdy tree and was climbing quite confidently until he got up to a branch about eight feet off the ground. Then he made a big mistake: he looked down. Suddenly, fear wrapped around him as tightly as he was wrapped around the limb. For what seemed like the longest time, he said he couldn't tell which way was up or down. And when Jim started up to rescue him, Tim began screaming.

No amount of coaxing from Jim or me could break through Tim's fear. Not knowing what else to do, I went after my father. When he came out of the house, he positioned himself directly on the ground beneath Tim and started speaking softly to him in a smooth, velvety voice. Gradually, my brother stopped screaming.

My father reached out his arms, but as long as they were, they still weren't quite long enough. There was only one thing that could cross that unbridgeable gap: earned trust. Dad had simply never failed us yet; he created, protected, and sustained our world. So when he said, "Jump, Timmy, go ahead and jump. I'll catch you!" Tim had the courage to strip himself away from the limb and jump into those long arms. He trusted his father even in the grip of paralyzing fear.

What is it that causes us to trust? Why do we trust some people less than others? And why, as a child in the long arms of my father, did I always feel so safe?

Trust, according to one dictionary, is a *firm reliance on the integrity, ability, or character of a person or thing.* This reliance, more often than not, is established over an extended period of time. Deep trust—the kind that convinces a six-year-old to leap from a tree—is the result of a track record. For as long as I can remember, and well before that, my father had shown himself trustworthy.

At birth I weighed only four pounds and two ounces and was a month premature. I would not take to my mother's breast and did not seem to have the strength to feed myself from a bottle. Night after night, my father stayed up with me, coaxing me to eat, watching me wrestle and then drop in weight until they thought they might lose me. He was the one who, with a pin, finally reached down and saved me. He made the hole on the end of the nipple much bigger and, from that one idea, sprung my life: I sucked and sucked, the milk flowing until it filled my stomach, my throat, my mouth, spilled over my lips, and flowed down my father's arm.

But that was just the beginning. In the years that followed, I brought to my father an endless parade of crippled trucks, amputated bears, skinned knees, broken dreams, and punctured tires. With a screwdriver or a bandage or a soft word, he could put to rest my worst fears and make me believe that things were never as bad as they appeared. I knew that there wasn't a place of potential loss or danger that he couldn't reach. I trusted him.

Part of that trust was the result of simply spending time with him. Unlike many fathers, my father let me into his life; he wanted me to be where he was. And in my father's presence, the most common places were often transformed into ones of mystery and magic.

Some of my earliest memories are of going along with my father to his work as nighttime delivery man, a second job which he had taken in anticipation of college bills. It was, in looking back, a strange job. On just one route, he would deliver such diverse and seemingly unrelated items as photographic film, mail, hamburger buns, and newspapers. As children, we never thought for one instant of the incongruity; the plain fact was that he always knew what he was doing.

Through towns with names like Mortimer, Pandora, Delphos, Lima, Leipsic, Kenton, Bluffton, Dunkirk, Ada, we would take the Ford Econoline van from train stations to post offices to photo labs to newspaper stands.

Through each town, in common or lonely or moon-kissed moments, there were always, in the shadow of my father, uncommon moments: listening to the way a train sounded, lonely and distant, on a summer night filled with dew; smelling the fresh cut of ink and newspaper, the way it stung and then played in the nose; watching the bulk of the mail bags piled impossibly onto one another on the wooden planks of U.S. Post Office delivery docks; fighting sleep while waiting for a pick-up at the B & J photo lab, mesmerized by the steady, red, neon blinking: J ... J ... J.... As hard as I might try to stay awake, I would drift off somewhere between two or three in the morning, half-conscious of the smell of idling fumes, the lights of towns, my father's arm slipping around me. It was a feeling of wild safety.

I would wake instinctively about 5 A.M. in Kenton, outside an old-fashioned bakery with wooden floors and smells which must be part of heaven. Grabbing a bale of newspapers in one hand and carrying me in his other arm, my father would place a quarter in my palm and lead me to a jelly donut. No matter how sleepy, I was always stunned by the warmth of the bakery and the way the donut would fall apart in my mouth, leaving in its wake a sweet, flaky, almost electric taste.

While my father's presence instilled the beginnings of my trust in him, his *power* is what secured that trust. After watching him work for a day, I truly believed there was nothing he could not do.

My father's primary job was working for the railroads. From 1946 until his retirement in 1988, he worked for the New York Central, the Nickel Plate, and the Norfolk & Western. For him, the railroad was more than just a job; it was a passion. To this day there is not a name of a rail line or railroad, either past or present, that he doesn't know by name. Cross a railroad and he will call it out—the DT&I, the old LE&W, the Chessie System, the T&OC, the Big Four of the New York Central, the AC&Y, the NKP—their marvelous and sturdy consonants and syllables slipping over his tongue in the rhythm of a train on its tracks. There isn't a locomotive, defunct or current, steam or diesel, that he cannot identify—the Berkshire (with a distinguishing 2–8–4 wheel arrangement), the Hudson (4–6–2 for less power, greater speed), the Mikado, the Pacific, the Alco diesel (nicknamed the Bluebird).

It was impossible not to associate the railroad with power, for there was power in nearly everything that came into contact with it. I can still close my eyes and see the locomotives shaking the ground and buildings as they passed by. I still remember the sturdy, simple names of the men—Bernie, Fritz, George, Vossie—that my father labored with.

And there was power, too, in the actual towers where my father worked. The towers were located by interchanges of railroads. At Maple Grove, the Pennsylvania and Nickel Plate railroads would cross, while Green Springs was a connection between the Big Four and the Nickel Plate. With each railroad controlling two sets of parallel tracks, there were, in each interchange, four "diamonds." In addition, there were also crossovers between parallel tracks that allowed trains to move from one track to another, and sidings where trains could be routed to allow other trains to pass through. Wherever railroads and tracks cross, of course, the traffic needed to be controlled and directed. Thus, the towers.

The buildings were square, constructed of burnt red concrete, and stood two stories tall in order to get the leverage needed to mechanically move switches and control interchanges. On the second floor, where men like my father worked, there were a collection of levers and switches. The levers, arranged side by side on the floor, were connected to long pivot rods, which extended like weird, iron tentacles through the first floor and connected to steel rods that mechanically moved the sections of tracks. The levers locked, sometimes with much effort and finesse, into place when thrown. The switches were smaller levers at eye level that electrically changed the train signals alongside the tracks to double red or yellow or green.

As a child, I was impressed with the mystery and steely charm of Maple Grove and Green Springs; I could feel their power surging around me. The place was wired with relays, batteries, and transformers that held enough voltage to throw whatever was needed for a loop. An electrical buzz, starting at a large black box outside the building, penetrated the wall of the stairs. It produced a steady hum that, even through concrete, crawled into your feet, shimmied up both legs, and spilled into your stomach and throat before settling into your subconscious like a mosquito during sleep.

Watching my father work was especially exciting as a train approached. First, he would take the train order over the dispatcher phone, crisply spelling aloud the destinations and towns and names. Then he would begin throwing switches and levers according to the diagram chart, his graceful, powerful motions sequenced according to direction and destination. He would, with a seamless set of motions, type a train order, throw a switch, align a signal, and watch for a distant light down the tracks.

Just as you could begin to feel the power of the approaching locomotive, my father would attach the paper he just typed to an "Iron Man," a Y-shaped device that allowed him to pass the train order to a man leaning out of the speeding train. Inside, the tower seemed to explode with the rhythm of sound, the rumble and shaking of the ground beneath, the ba-dump-da-dump of each car over the diamond, the slow, almost sad fading of the train into the distance. And then, bounding up the stairs, my father would return, smiling. To a child such a show of power was breathtaking, and the fact that he seemed to control it all generated a certain sense of awe.

In addition to his presence and power, my father also gained my trust by crafting and controlling my childhood world. There is no question in my mind that my dad was the beginning and end of whatever kingdoms my small hands could conceive.

There were, of course, the physical provisions. Only indirectly did we connect my father's work with those things he was able to provide. The greater effect of his work, I believe, was to elevate him in our eyes. We already thought of him as virtually indestructible because he could take our best punch and not even flinch, but the railroad confirmed what we always suspected: this man could even bring a speeding and powerful locomotive to its knees.

When my father was home he provided for us in a more direct way by reaching into our minds and plucking our most ripe desires. Piece by piece, he began to fashion a world around us: a sandbox, a tether ball pole, a swing on a giant oak's limb, a pony named Cocoa in what was once a chicken shed. He never stopped. With hammer and nail, a bag of concrete or dolomite, and a dumpload of imagination, our father gave us the mystical sense that the world, while impeccably safe, was never static and always exploding into surprise.

We never knew what to expect next. One year it was the four-foot deep above-the-ground pool where I learned to dive. The next year, it was our own private baseball field, angled against the railroad tie fence, lined with lime and anchored with makeshift bases. After that, it was a seven by twelve foot colonial style tree house with electricity, screened windows, two bunks, and a front porch.

But it was not just the things that were important. They always served as a means to another end, with the end always wild and impenetrable, like an unplugged balloon or the unleashing of imagination. The sandbox became a volcano; the swimming pool, a high dive; the tree house, a spy headquarters or an Apollo spacecraft.

Although I do remember my father playing with us—pushing us on swings, giving us rides on his back as he tried to buck us off, moving hand over hand to the tune of the Charleston as he pretended to make his knees cross one through the other—I don't remember him playing with us a great deal. Part of the art of my father's parenting skill was to create for us an environment, give us just enough of himself to pass for a hint or two, and let *us* play. He created for us our own world, really, one where we were safe and free to explore, imagine, and create. Such were the gifts of his love.

Certainly, there were boundaries. Tim and I knew them well, for when we went beyond my father-commanded limits, we found pain—either in terms of natural consequences or the dreaded "board of education." But neither the limitations nor the discipline in our world ever seemed mean-spirited or even particularly painful. Part of our acceptance of both was the almost instinctual knowledge, birthed and nurtured through experience, that our father knew what was best for us. With such an unshakable trust in my father—built on his power, presence and endless provision—each morning stretched out before me in grace, wonder, and possibility.

I learned many of the characteristics of a good father from my earthly father. With all the power he could muster, he created for us a world of security, play, freedom, discipline, and grace. With his presence, he gave us the wonder and magic of leaving us longing for his hug, his acceptance, his love. And with his provision, he gave us not only what we needed to survive, such as food and shelter, but also created for us a world filled with imagination, peace, adventure, creativity, and love. In such an environment we did not just exist, but matured and prospered.

Still, as great as these demonstrations of my father's love were, they are nothing compared to the love of the Father in heaven. Matthew 23:9 says, "And do not call anyone on earth 'father,' for you have one Father, and he is in heaven."

In my mind, it is no accident that God is called Father: He is the ultimate provider, sustainer, giver of good gifts, discipliner, lover, creator. He is all-encompassing, all-powerful, all-loving. In his power, presence, and provision, he is not simply an abstract and good Being; his very name, "Father," implies an intense and intimate relationship. In a primal way, he exists in the reality of his children, for if he had no children, he would cease to be a Father. He is that deeply tied into us.

According to Ephesians 3:20, God is "able to do immeasurably more than all we ask or imagine, according to his power that is at work in us." There is no crisis or need, no desire or challenge or hope that cannot be met through God's provision and power. Unlimited by perspective, sin, weakness, or fear, his love for his children simply knows no bounds. He will stop at nothing to demonstrate his love for us. He asks only for our trust.

When I think of the ultimate trust of a child, I am reminded of Jesus on a tree in the shape of a cross. Nails prevented Jesus, the son of the Father, from jumping; darkness kept his Father from his sight. Death was just a painful breath or two away as he cried, "My God, my God, why have you forsaken me!" What sort of hell was this breaking loose? Just what kind of leap did the Father have in mind?

For it had been through the Father that Jesus had always broken free. Completely abandoning himself to his Father's will and protection, Jesus had always seemed remarkably free and full of life. It hurt some people, the careful ones, to watch him. They thought, after all, that life was a matter of preserving, cultivating, fearing—all those things that caused them little joy and such great exhaustion. But here was the son of God, who, trusting in his Father, spoke of giving, dying, breathing, loving. "Seek first my Father's will and there will be no need for fear or worry," Jesus had urged. "See life as a gift from the Father and give yourself away. Does not the Father clothe even the lilies, most of them unseen? Will he not wrap his very own children in love and protection and the king's clothes?"

And then, just as he had lived, Jesus died. Beyond the grave, beyond the wrath, beyond the separation, beyond all hell itself, God, unseen and unheard through the great final abyss, asked his son to trust him one final time. To jump. And Jesus did, landing in the long unseen arms of his Father.

> But we see Jesus, who was made a little lower than the angels, now crowned with glory and honor because he suffered death, so that by the grace of God

he might taste death for everyone. In bringing many sons to glory, it was fitting that God, for whom and through whom everything exists, should make the author of their salvation perfect through suffering. Both the one who makes men holy and those who are made holy are of the same family. So Jesus is not ashamed to call them brothers. He says, "I will declare your name to my brothers; in the presence of the congregation I will sing your praises." And again, "I will put my trust in him." And again he says, "Here am I, and the children God has given me." (Hebrews 2:9–13)

We, the other people who call God Father, often have such little trust. Jumping out of bed is often a frightening enough ordeal. In our day-to-day reality we, more often than not, rely on our own puny strength to realize our dreams, feed our family or, more likely, just get by. Isn't it ironic that we worry about the orthodontist's bill when in just one breath of God there is more power than if all of the atoms in the cosmos were split at once?

What can we do then to develop a deeper trust? The answer, I believe, is contained in Jesus' words that we must change and become like little children. Trust is inherently child-like, laced with a raw and open spirit of anticipation, wonder, and love. By contrast, adults— hidden in layers of fear, protected by logic, and shattered by broken dreams—are often cut off from the true qualities of trust.

But we must be careful in methodology. If, in our desire to become more like little children, we ask for a twelve-step program called *From Forty to Four*, we have missed the point, for this is the linear, sequential action of an adult. Instead of steps—carefully measured and anchored to a one-dimensional *doing*—we must rediscover what it means to *be* like children.

Children's trust, for example, is birthed in the fact of their helplessness. Without their daddy and mommy, there would be no food, no toys, no existence. Their dependence on others is so deep there is no separation in their minds between the air that they breathe and the existence of their parents; it goes without saying—or even conscious thought—that both are necessary.

Adults, on the other hand, often pride themselves on their independence. By creating narrow and efficient worlds, they seek control and self-sufficiency. Cut off from the largeness of the world, they lose perspective. There is simply no reason for trust in such a disconnected state.

So perspective must be regained. A walk under the stars, reflection on the Psalms "... as for man, his days are like grass ...," times of solitude to allow the blurring motion of busyness to unravel, or a visit to a grandfather's grave can help restore the proper measure of man, earth, and God, revealing once again the necessity of trust.

Also inherent in child-like trust is an open mind and heart. Because they have not been taught the difference between what is possible and impossible, children are uniquely qualified for miracles. When my father did the

Charleston, crossing one knee through the other, I chose amazement over doubt.

Adults, however, are quite clear on what is possible and what is not because their world is calculated through logic and mathematics. In such a closed system, their hearts and minds shut down. Paychecks and budgets and two-year plans become the heavily defended borderlines of their existence. Trust comes only in certain sizes.

Child-like trust in God demands that adults unlearn what we think about possibility: "I can do all things through Christ...."; "with God all things are possible ...."; "the God of glory thunders, the Lord, upon many waters." We need to reimagine the qualities of God outside the parameters and standards of man. Because the chasm between God and man is so great, we must seek to bridge the gap with hints of his majesty, power, holiness, self-giving, wrath, and love in an ever-impassioned desire to expand our minds and hearts.

I am very fortunate to have the father of my childhood to reflect, even so dimly, the qualities of my heavenly Father. When my father would throw the switches and levers, tripping electricity and steel and directing and moving the incredible motion and mass of fierce locomotives, he seemed so powerful to me. How much more, then, can I trust the power of my heavenly Father, who created and possesses the power of a billion exploding suns?

For those not raised in the care of a loving father, other people and events can provide hints of God's characteristics. When was the last time you stopped to watch a thunderstorm move across a field or a lake, moving you in awe of God's power? Or stood close to a fire and felt the heated passion, a hint of the energy of God's holiness? What about the way a mother cradles her sick child, stirring in your heart the endless compassion of God?

Trust is no small thing. It means leaving all we have in the hands of God. It means dying to our needs to control, manipulate, and order our own world. It means imagining a reality larger than our own fears and lives. From our earthly perspective—warped in time, sin, and death—being asked to trust God is no easy matter; it is the same awareness a child has while dangerously hanging from a tree saying, "Daddy, I can't get down." But when we do trust enough to jump, we do so with the knowledge and assurance that we will land safely in our Father's loving arms.

3 WONDER

He who can no longer pause to wonder and stand rapt in awe, is as good as dead; his eyes are closed.

ALBERT EINSTEIN 🖂

As a child I was never prepared for twilight, that brief period of time between the setting of the sun and the fall of night when light and darkness merge in slow motion. I knew it would come, falling with the force and color of a rose petal, but I never seemed to notice the light slip into a pastel spectrum on the horizon and then slowly die, fading into whispers of turquoise, indigo, violet, and midnight blue. More times than not twilight stunned me, spilling into my consciousness in a rushing, racing moment. There were times when the force of such a softly echoing sunset settled into my lungs, my feet, and my memory, leaving me breathless and motionless.

I remember one hot July evening especially. In the field across from my grandpa's ancient brick house bats from nearby attics and caverns fluttered like butterflies at impossible angles, their squeaking like the sound of doors in the night and creaking porch swings. The night air held a kind of dampness, beading on windows, pooling in blue-gray fog, settling on voices.

Tim and I, along with some cousins, had been exploring one of the back rooms of my grandfather's house. The room had never been used for much, and over the years it had collected dust, detective magazines, old cigar boxes, broken bits of dolls and fans and HO-scale model trains. The room always left me feeling dizzy with its closed-in smells and resistance to the present tense, and I tumbled out into the falling night slightly disoriented.

My brother and cousins remained behind. I heard a muffled laugh, maybe a trapped exclamation, and wondered for a second what sort of treasure they might have found. And then I fell into the silence. I stood still, listening, breathing, not thinking, not moving, and then seeing, but not *just* seeing.

Across the street in the field and extending deep into the valley were thousands of them, ridiculous in their brilliance. Fireflies. I had seen them before—beat them with my yellow plastic bat until it glowed in the dark, stuffed them into a jar and released them into my bedroom—but this was altogether different, a never before seen and never again to be repeated event.

The fireflies spread a blanket of light into the deepening purple of twilight—an eternity of green-yellow eruptions, like bits of lightning taught to fly and hover and draft and blink one by one by one. Eruptions of chemicals and instinct, scientists would say, but I knew in the way the night was pricked thousands and thousands of times that this was magical. I stood and watched transfixed until, from behind, I felt my mother's arms wrap around me, her whisper producing the same sense of wonder in me as the fireflies before us.

My mother. If my father was the constant creator of my childhood world, my mother was its spirit. I have difficulty freezing her into any particular moment because she was simply always there—feeding, helping, teaching, being, touching, encouraging. To try to recall specific incidents would be like removing a glass of water from a river and calling it the river: the essential flow is missing.

There were some constants, however. My mother was distinctly feminine, with large, wonder-filled brown eyes and dark brown hair that toyed with the idea of being black. The sense of mystery about her was generally offset by the way she held herself, slender and petite, with a steady sense of humility or maybe amusement.

She was partial to red, I think, without knowing it and wore the color with surprising grace, formally or casually, with a button-down sweater or a matching skirt and coat or a pair of ridiculous sunglasses. And that same sort of flexibility and passion went beyond her clothes; she also wore it in her disarming ability to laugh or pose or comfort. I never knew anyone who did not like my mother.

My mother's sense of wonder sprang from her attitude about life. In her perplexing balance of passion and composure, she never seemed to sacrifice doing for being; in fact, her actions seemed to flow unconsciously out of who she was, and I always had the impression that she loved in much the same fashion as she breathed. There was always a subtle and dynamic energy in her, leaking out in the most startling and singular ways: the way she bandaged a finger, flavored noodles, or told the story of Jonah.

And finally, like many other people blessed with the wondrous ability to see God in the color of an autumn leaf or in the dirtiest children, my mother was humble; she knew her place in the grander scheme of things and it was seldom center stage. Through instinct and a growing relationship with God, she somehow managed to be fully alive and yet unobtrusive in much the same way that Christ, slipping in and out of crowds, was sometimes mistaken for a gardener or a traveler.

Because it was so much a part of her, it is not surprising that a sense of wonder was my mother's greatest gift to me. It was she who showed me that wonder was not just an attribute, like calling a house yellow, but an undergirding attitude, a compass pointed toward God. She did this in conscious ways by laughing with her eyes, or giving way to silence. Her sense of wonder, like seeds in a garden, sprung from the dirt of reality— a strawberry, a sunset, a lipstick kiss.

But her sense of wonder was even more, I think, in who she was. She was never obsessed or addicted or hurried, like those ladies in sitcoms or shopping malls, but was rooted in something beyond herself. Her life demonstrated the principle of John 15:5: "I am the vine; you are the branches. If a man remains in me and I in him, he will bear much fruit; apart from me you can do nothing."

❦

Wonder is difficult to describe. As it usually is with such obstinate and irreducible words, its dictionary definition is ambiguous: *Something strange or surprising; a cause of surprise, astonishment, or admiration,* states Webster's. Another dictionary adds *awe* to the list; still another suggests the word *marvel.* Samuel Johnson said that "all wonder is the effect of novelty on ignorance." Another great thinker wrote nearly the opposite: "As knowledge increases, wonder deepens."

Can you sense the groping here? To me, it is not surprising that wonder is so immune to words. After all, if you could define wonder, dismantle it like the gears in a watch, where would the wonder be? Like an atom, the word is elemental, thriving on its inherent power, the tension between opposing forces. Break it down any further, and you have a problem the size of Hiroshima.

Wonder is equally resistant to a single concept. Some people call it more of an attitude; others would say a perspective; still others, a skill or a gift. These are all true, or course, but each misses the mark. I suspect that the best one can do is to describe the environment in which wonder exists, just as Paul did when he defined faith by speaking of pilgrims, martyrs, and the poor in spirit. Only by understanding certain characteristics of people who are wonder-filled, like my mother, is it possible to come to grips with the *process* of wonder, if not its concrete, static meaning. For wonder, like faith, is always moving, always free.

My mother, as I have stated before, was a person who was always rooted in something beyond herself, whether that was God, her husband, or her children. In her Spirit-fed humility, she instinctively understood that self, with its gripping tentacles of need and demand, was never satisfied, always grasping for something beyond its reach or capability. But because my mother was unanchored to self, she was free to give herself fully to others—to listen, to see, to touch, to connect, to respond.

She was also free to be who she was—a woman loved and provided for by God himself. To simply *be*. Because she did not look at time as something to be hoarded in the vain hope of redeeming it for something better in the future, she was free to live in the now. And now, in every moment, is always where wonder happens.

I love the verse in John that speaks of this mysterious and penetrating freedom: "The wind blows wherever it pleases. You hear its sound, but you cannot tell where it comes from or where it is going. So it is with everyone born of the Spirit" (John 3:8). There is wonder in the moving of the wind and in the openness of possibility. That's the way it was with my mother: there was always the unspoken and unconscious expectation that something was about to break into reality. And it usually did. She always seemed to make things happen or, at the very least, found herself somewhere near the middle of all that fell, leaped, danced, bounced, or spilled. Given her charisma, the right era, and a black pair of boots, she could have been anything from a silent film star to a rainmaker.

She also had an uncanny knack and rhythm for happenstance. While some people might wrongly confuse this knack as good luck or dumb luck or bad luck or no luck, it should never be mistaken for the nucleated grace that I believe it actually was. A sense of wonder, I have come to believe, breeds wonders: She just couldn't help herself. Although I never recall her slipping on something as obvious as a banana peel, she would slide on a word, a circumstance, or a sideways glance and become the center for hilarity or release.

Part of my mom's uncanny ability to make people laugh was her unpretentious nature. One example was her clumsy and stubborn tongue. Try as she would, even clucking and curling and rolling and clicking, no amount of exercise or gumption could force it to perform as she wanted. For instance, it is a commonly known fact in my family that my mother never said "Detroit" in two syllables. Whenever she tried, it came out with an extra syllable: "De-troy-it." She could try to say it slowly, quickly, with enunciation or without, laced with a heavy accent, or think of other similar words such as "the ploy" or "bee toy" or "free boy" (all of which she *could* say), but when it came down to the crunch, there it was, as unintended as a missing shoe: "De-troy-it.

This made her a favorite target for tongue twisters. Maybe it was just my youthful ignorance, but I swear that entire parties were thrown, catered, and themed around my mother's tongue. ("Come one, come all.

Evelyn Wilkins will give her interpretation of Peter Piper, She Sells Sea Shells, and How Much Wood Could a Woodchuck Chuck? along with all your other favorites.")

But words weren't her worst beasts. My mother also had a kind of weird rapport with animals. Although I never considered her particularly to be an animal lover—"will you oil that stupid hamster wheel?" was about as close as she came to fanaticism concerning the animal kingdom—she seemed to share with them a certain kineticism, a wild-eyed and grazing perspective on certain issues.

One incident especially sticks in my mind. Our pony, Cocoa, was a strange pony to be sure, what with drinking water out of a hose and Pepsi out of a bottle, but he tended to get even odder around my mother. This particular afternoon Tim and I had been riding Cocoa and dismounted him by the porch steps in order to join the rest of our family who had gathered on the front porch. A few minutes later, Cocoa decided he too wanted to be part of the party. Carefully managing each of the four steps like a pot-bellied ballerina, he walked casually into our midst. He was, in fact, so nonchalant about his movements that no one even said a word, as if a pony on a front porch was as customary and expected as a sunrise. We continued talking.

As was his custom, Cocoa began edging toward my mother, who was sitting on the porch swing. In retrospect, we should have seen it coming. What with the easy success of his entrance onto the porch and the way his eyes were glossing over with a sense of tranquillity, his next move was simply an extension of logic or—dare I say it?—good old-fashioned horse sense.

Backing up slowly and methodically, like a train in reverse, he made his approach, his head tilted carefully over his shoulder. As he began to bend his rear knees, my mother, blessed with a certain amount of horse sense of her own, quickly calculated the size of the wrong end of the horse that was now approaching her, measured it against the size of the porch swing and, although she was never particularly a whiz at math, knew immediately it was an equation for a potential disaster.

Leaping, screaming, and whacking horse butt at the same time, she narrowly averted an embarrassing visit to the doctor's office. ("Well, Mrs. Wilkins, how did these splinters get . . . hem, hem . . . a . . . well, here?") Cocoa was startled—I sincerely believe he was expecting no opposition to his desire to sit down—and not only abandoned his plan but the front porch as well. My mother, allowing for a few moments to jettison the image of a pony sitting in her lap, returned to the swing, laughed, and resumed talking about finger painting or cheerleader tryouts or my uncle's failing heart or something like that.

That is the sort of attraction my mother held. Animals, events, and moments seemed drawn to her. So were people, especially those labeled "losers." Growing up, I remember our house as a refuge for outcasts of society such as Earl, an effeminate teenager who had no friends; Linda, a hard-as-rock forty-year-old who everyone considered a little cracked; and Joel, an over-weight eight-year-old with contact lenses who could not stop blinking back the tears. These and others could always be found somewhere in my mother's wake. I believe this was wonder in its most precious and rare form. Like a skilled surgeon, my mother could cut through someone's pain, ridicule, and despair to extract a laugh, a hope, a new friend. She saw, in the most damaged, hurting people, the flash of the image of God.

I once went fishing with a man on a lake at night. With only the stars for light, we smoked cigars as we cast our lines into the water. The darkness was everywhere; it was impossible to tell where the water, land, and horizon began or ended. I had the chills even though it was warm.

I thought he would say something about the eerieness, but he just went on and on in a thoughtless chatter as though he was on his living room couch or riding in a car—completely oblivious to the fact that we were being swallowed by darkness. This man lived a life filled with addiction and obsession and thought it the norm: he moved from houseplants to beer to racquet-ball to cars to softball, even trying his hand at religion. "Everyone has to have a hobby," he used to say. I'm not even sure what he talked about on this particular night, no doubt the jargon of his latest kick. I was aware of only one thing: he never looked at the stars.

I have often wondered about those who never won-der. I had planned to talk to him about God that night, but if a night sky full of stars meant nothing to him, what good would a few words do? It was almost as if this man, like a deaf or a blind person, lacked functioning sense organs. The dullness was frightening.

What had cut short his ability to wonder? Perhaps it was because the man had no father or mother and was moved back and forth from orphanage to foster home until he was finally adopted at the age of twelve. He was never allowed to be a child, free and timeless and won-der-filled. Instead, to him childhood was simply a place of survival; time, the clicking of the hours until the next home; trust, what you did for the next meal; wonder, those irrelevant stirrings in the heart.

Without wonder, did he simply wither up and die? Will the transcendent and eternal realities of God, spirit, hope, faith ever compare, in his stunted mind, to the Chicago Bears or a new garden tractor or fishing on a night lake for thirteen small-mouthed bass? And can he be blamed, really, if he prefers what is here and now for what seems always far and away?

When my car broke down on that Illinois highway on the cement outskirts of Chicago, I too felt overwhelmed by responsibility, duty, and anxiety. Neck-deep into my own adult life, it was only when I saw my two-year-old son dancing among the dandelion seeds that it struck me that I had lost my sense of wonder. How long had it been since I listened to the electrical scrapings of crickets and grasshoppers in an August evening? How long since I saw the way light fell on telephone wires and church steeples in the cool, long distance of early morning? How long had

I passed over the crook, just like my wife's, in my little boy's smile? How long had it been since I had listened, really listened, to that still, small voice?

I had abandoned what my mother had taught me. I had my reasons, of course. I was doing things, important things, even godly things. The world was going to hell, after all, and it was up to me to stand against the flow of the Styx. There was simply no time or energy to waste on wonder. But in my busyness, I no longer had time to just *be*. In all of my doing, I lost sight of the world: its slow arcs of blue and green, the way a hill fell against the sky, the voice in the throat of a stream, the dancing of shadows, and, through all of it, the wildness of grace.

In the blur of my doing, I had also lost sight, finally, of God. With my sense of wonder destroyed, God simply became someone to fit into my daytimer next to the lunch with H. James or the reminder to call CompuServe. When wonder dies, the mind is truncated, its synapses bound mercilessly to the dimension of logic. In that distortion of mind, God ceases to be someone beyond understanding. Instead of being the center and flow of the universe, he is reduced to doctrine and calculation, which, when you think about it, is nothing more than the graphite in a pencil.

Once God is reduced, the possibilities for faith and abundant life are nearly destroyed. Without wonder, faith is reduced to religion, the sacred to familiarity, the living Word to dogma. Out of the ensuing boredom, Christianity becomes nothing more than the definitions of a club (klub) n. **1.** A stout, heavy stick used to beat heathens into submission. **2.** A group of people organized around a common purpose, i.e., ending abortion. Without wonder, we find *ourselves* orphans, disconnected from the Father.

❦

When it comes to developing wonder, each of us has choices. By its very definition, wonder is immune to formula, strategy, technique; the second you try to capture it is the same moment you will never find it. My mother did not consciously start each day by saying, "I'm going to be amazed at the world today." She simply gave notice to what was already there.

Wonder cannot be controlled, but we *may* choose to pay attention. G. K. Chesterton wrote, "The world will never starve for want of wonders, but for want of wonder." On nearly any August night, deep in impossibly green valleys, fireflies still pierce the night. In each garden turned by human hand, fruits and vegetables are still birthed. Around each life, stunted and hopeless people still wait to surprise us with the flickering image of God. In the everyday and *common* things of creation and grace, there are wonders. The question is whether we have the eyes to see and ears to hear.

Or do we got lost in the blur and noise of doing? In order to encourage wonder, we must not confuse the rush of endorphins—the enduring addiction of always doing, doing, doing—with a sense of purpose. Well-being depends mostly upon *being* well.

I can hear the objections: Time is money. I have responsibilities. My family has needs. The world is going to hell, and I must do all that I can. Devoid of wonder, we get the strange and logical view that nearly everything depends upon us. *Need* is warped by our flat perspective: I *need* that job; our child *needs* this computer class; my wife *needs* to teach Sunday school. Priorities get shuffled, and once again we become busy at life and sacrifice wonder, the core of all there is. We close our ears to the small voice of the One who says, "Trust me, I love you. I alone can and will meet your needs."

But here is the paradox. It is only in the inertia of simply *being* that we will find the motivation and energy necessary for doing. This, too, I learned from my mother. When I was a child, she had a knack for helping me gently rise from sleep to awareness, speaking softly, sliding a hand over my shoulder or back, drawing me from the prism of a dream into the clear light of morning. Sometimes I would sit up, still in the fog that follows sleep, and we would sit wordlessly by the edge of the bed. Here, in the warmth and presence of my mother, the spirit of my world, I would awake to another morning, to the endless and childlike realm of possibility awaiting me.

So often, we adults have lost this ability to just *be*. To regain it, we must slow down and expand our world: taste, smell, touch, listen, see. Then rent a houseboat on a remote lake and hear the voice of God in the night call of the whippoorwill. Or spend some time with the lonely boy down the street, looking for the flash of a smile. Or take some friends on a mid-afternoon picnic and really listen to what they have to say. You may be surprised at the sense of wonder reawakened inside you.

4 *FEAR*

The timidity of the child or the savage is entirely reasonable; they are alarmed at this world, because this world is a very alarming place. They dislike being alone because it is verily and indeed an awful idea to be alone.

G. K. CHESTERTON 🌿

I remember the fear. In the dead of winter I would awake, windows howling in the wind, bare branches of a tree scraping the glass of my bedroom window with thin, arthritic fingers. To this day, I can still see the shadows dancing on my bedroom walls—the weightlessness of their frenetic movements, the varying shades of black, the whispers I was sure were there, but could never quite hear. Sometimes I would bolt upright in my bed, eyes wide in terror. Other times, pillow over my head, I would pull the blankets tightly around me and bury myself in fear.

To add to this fear, I experienced a period in my childhood where my senses seemed disorted. I would wake up in the middle of the night frying in the adrenaline of terror, unable to orient myself. In the gray-black darkness, my vision would be distorted and filled with fog, and even close objects appeared distant, almost as if in another dimension.

Stormy nights were the worst. Sometimes I would call for my father. I would see him coming, way in the distance, and then, in the next second, right on top of me. The lightning falling on his face created an unearthly glow. The trees scraping the windows mixed with the words coming from his mouth. There seemed to be an uncrossable chasm between us. "The windows aren't howling," my father would try to explain, "they are vibrating in the wind." Or "Trees don't have fingers; it's just the limbs being blown against the glass." And then he would hug me, kiss me on the cheek, and stumble back to bed, his words trailing behind him: "You see, son? There's nothing to be afraid of." And then I was alone again with my fear.

I'll never forget the impression those nights had on me. Not only was it the static terror of the fear itself, but also the terror of disillusionment: My father, who had always been able to protect me before, stumbling back to sleep, leaving me alone up against something only I could sense. When I read Jesus' words about hell—"And throw that worthless servant outside, into the darkness, where there will be weeping and gnashing of teeth" (Matthew 25:30)—my mind always moves back to waking up alone in the middle of the night.

But childhood fears do not live only in nighttime bedrooms. Because we lived in the country, every so often a farmer would plant corn in the field right behind our backyard. This was always a treat for us, for, unlike other crops, corn was hearty and grew rapidly; to a child, a field of corn stopped just short of a whole new forest.

Every August that we had corn to play in Tim and I would make a game of taking turns walking into the corn and then returning. Each time, we would dare each other to move farther into the cornfield. What I didn't know then was that Tim possessed a good sense of direction—I did not. However, I did not like to lose, not even an innocent little game, so on about my fifth turn I decided to go farther than either of us had ever gone before; farther, in fact, than any boy had ever gone into a cornfield at any time in the history of the known world. With determination, I walked and walked and walked, eventually hearing my brother's voice fade into nothing. When I thought I had walked far enough, I forced myself to walk some more. I stopped, turned around, and just as the pride of winning struck me, I realized I was lost.

I panicked, as six-year-olds are prone to do, and then, not possessing the steadiness of mind to retrace my steps or follow a single row of corn in one direction, ran back and forth, here and there, slowly at first, then as fast as I could. The leaves of corn sliced into my skin with a steady, rasping sound and, with each new step, a prickly rush of adrenaline spread over my body like coarse wool.

After about fifteen minutes, I tired and stood still. In each direction, as far as I could see, rows of corn headed off into infinity. In my excited state of mind, I began to

take notice of all the movement: the thousands of dancing plants, the motion of the wind, my heavy breathing,
the sun peeking back and forth through the tufted plants,
throwing shadows like quick, livid darts. And down there,
fifteen or twenty rows down, what was that?

I was aware too—above, beyond, and in my fear—
that I was lost. Alone, with no way home. I called for my
brother and, at first, could only manage a coarse whisper. His name, ever so softly, seemed to move down the
field like a tumbleweed—Tim . . . *Tim* . . . *Tim* . . . *Ti* . . .
T . . . and I was left alone again. The next time I yelled a
little louder; his name seemed to skip faster from me;
finally, I managed a scream which seemed to disappear
instantly, followed by nothing, not even an echo.

Alone. I am not sure how long I stayed in the cornfield, but I remember praying, finding control, consciously arranging the wild firing of sparks in my head,
and settling my fear into a slow, steady buzzing. At least I
was able to think, if not always in a straight line. I moved
deliberately, one foot after the other, in one direction.

After a few minutes, I heard something in the distance—what I thought to be of a slightly different texture than the slash of corn leaves. A few seconds later it
was clearer—voices? I stood still and listened intently,
opening my ears as wide as they had ever been before.
There it was again: the voices of my mother and my
brother. With all my might, I ran toward those voices,
and then, after a minute or so, toward the light of day. I
was crying when I spilled out of the cornfield into my
mother's arms: lost and then found.

❧

A child's fear is a purely elemental, no-holds-barred, undistracted form of terror, unlimited by motives, contributing factors, or pride. Experiencing fear as an adult is not the same—never as bright, paralyzing, or sane— as when you are a child. For one thing, the fear is usually diluted by something else. Fear of a terrible illness, for example, is mixed with a sense of selfishness—I will miss out on *this* or *that;* fear at losing a job is convoluted with anger toward my boss; fear of being stung by a bee is tempered by a sense of embarrassment at having to hop about on one foot.

Adults also consciously try to submerge or control fear. This, of course, is done in a number of ways, not the least of which is advertising: "Buy Michelins and you won't have to fear your children being involved in an automobile accident." "Take antioxidants or eat broccoli and you won't have to fear cancer." "Invest through this broker and you will never have to worry about money in the future."

Another approach in dealing with fear that tends to be favored by the male population is pretending to ignore it. About four years ago, my wife and I were driving from Chicago to Pensacola, Florida, to visit my parents. My parents had recently moved there, and this was our first trip to see them in their new home. According to the map, the quickest route seemed to be to get off I–65—a four-lane major interstate—and follow Routes 31 and 87 through what remained of Alabama and into the panhandle of Florida.

What I could not foresee, however, was that Routes 31 and 87 cut through some of the most abandoned and desolate places in the country. I remember mostly how dark it was; once, I got out of my car with a rag to wipe the headlights. We drove for miles and miles with nothing—no stores, no houses, no streetlights, absolutely nothing. To make matters worse, I had only an eighth of a tank of gas, and, from my calculations, we had another sixty miles to go.

But this was not even the most alarming part of the trip. When we finally did come upon a gas station—a lonely, dilapidated building with one gasping streetlight—did I stop? No, I was too proud. By the timbre of her voice, I could tell my wife was near panic, thinking we would run out of gas. "No problem," I said as we breezed past the station, "we have plenty of gas. Besides, it's too expensive." Somewhere near the dawning of civilization we made it to the next station, but I never did tell my wife that we were literally running on fumes.

On the whole, humanity has done a remarkable job of ignoring or eliminating the most basic fears. Through our creations of civilization, technology, medicine, tools, and any number of inventions, we have buffered ourselves into far less disturbing realities.

A few years ago, I was writing a story on a missionary who worked on a Navajo Indian reservation in the high deserts of New Mexico. Traveling there, I was immediately impressed with the pull of the land—its wild, almost desperate beauty, its sturdy and improbable formations of rock, the sky that seemed always in violent transition.

Yet what really stunned me was the purity of the darkness at night without electricity; it fell over the earth like the ocean swallows pebbles, leaving only an oily black pierced brightly with stars and an unshakable loneliness. This fear was fresh and real, not the kind of lingering, anxiety-fed fear of most adults but overwhelming in its presence, instinctive, plunging to the bone.

In another and more subtle sense, my fear as a child was the opposite of aloneness. It was more of an awareness, really, like seeing shadows in the dark or thinking that I was surrounded by things too frightful for the imagination. Children, of course, are famous for such creatures—monsters under the bed, ghosts at the window, boogey-men in the closet.

One of my earliest memories of childhood was being put down for a nap at my grandfather's house. My parents set up the crib in a room that was only occasionally used. Although I fell asleep quickly, I awoke about an hour later feeling some kind of odd and cold presence. For some reason, I began staring at the grain of the wood in the door. Suddenly—and I remember this like it was yesterday— the grain took on the appearance of a wolf and, leaping from its one dimension, jumped toward me in my crib. Even with her most reassuring hugs and words, it took an hour for my mother to calm me.

It is a peculiar and enduring quality of childhood that most children believe there *are* things that go bump in the night, that move in the dance of leaves, that break upon each of us at unexpected moments. For the child, these interruptions are as much a part of reality as a favorite stuffed animal.

I have a friend who has a three-year-old girl named Sarah. Recently, Sarah has been having trouble going to sleep; shortly after she is put to bed, she cries out for her daddy. "There is an alligator in my room," Sarah informs her dad. One night, in an effort to calm Sarah, her daddy came into the room with an imaginary gun, firing imaginary shots at what he considered to be an imaginary alligator. "There, Sarah," he confidently said to his daughter, "I shot the alligator dead." Sarah was unconvinced. "But, Daddy," she said, "you need to get your real gun because this is a real alligator."

Anchored in our rationality, we chuckle. Certainly, there is no real alligator. Then, based on the evidence of our five senses, we patiently explain to our children our logic, the movement of linear reason. But sometimes I wonder if we, as adults, just overlook the wildness of things. In our day-to-day, mixed-up world of carpets, deception, air-conditioning, RV campers, numbness, picket fences, and resignation, I can't help but think that we have disconnected ourselves from the fear we knew as children. After all, why would we want to remind ourselves of, let alone experience, such primal and over-powering forces?

Many of us may remember, as children, such moments of pure terror that we confuse the pounding of our heart for only what is bad. But fear is designed to be a good thing. What if none of us ever sensed fear? Would we not become self-destructive, engaging in any number of wildly erratic behaviors such as petting cobras or jumping from trees? Fear, in its purest sense, is designed as an alarm or a reminder; it teaches us to know our place and it provides perspective.

The Bible says that the fear of the Lord is the beginning of wisdom. In fear that is pure, I think there is always a hook into the fear of the Lord. Look at the fear of being alone—the helplessness of being disconnected from others. Isn't this simply a recognition of our abandonment in the cosmos and the nerve-shattering realization that, by ourselves, we are forever separated from God? And the fear of never being alone—isn't it the instinctual awareness of a teeming reality which we cannot see?

And these fears do harbor truth; left by ourselves, we *are* separated and vulnerable. But it is to the fear of the Lord, if all goes well, that these childlike fears will bring us. In fear, we see the correct perspective of the universe: without a god, there simply is no hope.

But even *a* god will never do. The only god that can bring hope to the world is the God with a capital G as tall as the cosmos, the God who is more powerful than all other unseen forces in the world and who can bridge the immeasurable separation between himself and man. This God, on whom we are utterly dependent, must be a source of fear that overwhelms and humbles. With him, all other fears are swallowed and diminished. This kind of fear, in more than one sense, is wonder driven to the next step.

People of faith in the Bible had a cultivated and natural fear of God. The ancient Israelites, for example, never uttered the name *Yahweh* for fear of being struck dead on the spot. They asked Moses to be their mediator because the thought of standing alone before a holy God turned their knees into manna-flavored Jell-O. Each person who came into the presence of the holy and glorified God buried his face in the dirt. "Woe is me for I am undone," Isaiah cried out before God, "for I am a man of unclean lips."

Where is the fear of God today? Virtually non-existent. Yet, paradoxically, another kind of fear has come to dominate our culture—not fear in its pure and natural state but a fear corrupted by being wrapped around sin. Never before in the history of man has there been more gadgets and self-defense tools to keep people safe: movement-sensitive security systems, mace, Judo, electric fences, police departments, specially bred dogs.

Incredibly, all this fear has not led us to God. Even Christians, who sing about trust on Sunday mornings, refuse to come into God's presence and hear the words "Do not be afraid." Instead, we either cower or coil. We are often reduced to believing that the world is depending on each one of us to handle the danger through a correct formula of caution, logic, and manipulation. I know many devoted Christians who, either consciously or unconsciously, believe that we have a *responsibility* to handle danger—that is why God made us logical, functional, and confident people.

Such an aggressive, self-dependent approach clearly underestimates the depth of danger that each of us is in. While we can certainly buy guns to eliminate prowlers, can we really do anything about the cancer cells that may be forming in one of our loved one's bodies? We can install fire alarms in our houses, but can we quench the finality of certain and sometimes sudden death? No matter how hard we try to deal completely with danger, there will always be the certainty of trouble. Jesus said, "Do not be afraid of those who kill the body but cannot kill the soul; rather, be afraid of the One who can destroy both soul and body in hell" (Matthew 10:28).

Control is probably the most common way people handle fear. Because of the wildness of fear and its immense ability to unsettle us, there is a tendency to reduce, manage, or ignore it. Instead of driving us to God in dependency, we try to tame fear ourselves.

In the journey from childhood to adulthood, we learn about control in all areas of our lives. As we interact with our environment we develop skills so that we are no longer always subject to the whims and actions of others. We learn how to roast hot dogs, conjugate verbs, hit nails, take showers, and attract spouses. Because fear is so powerful, we learn the skills necessary to deal with it as well.

But there is always a catch to this approach. Because of our inevitable failure to handle danger, we fight circular battles. In an effort to eliminate fear, we end up exhausted, feeling pressured and unable to take risks. Our lives are reduced to anger, manipulation, self deception, and, ultimately, futility.

At the opposite extreme of those who feel they must take an aggressive stance toward danger are those who advocate a fatalistic surrender to fear. This too is a form of control, albeit rather backward. These people believe that, no matter what they do, danger will most certainly catch up with them. Why hold on to any hope at all? This kind of fear comes clothed in apathy, numbness, and resignation. Christians who take this attitude toward danger isolate themselves from the world, attempting to build a cocoon around themselves in order to stay safe.

In either case, the result is the same: instead of us controlling fear, fear controls us. As one philosopher wrote, "If a man harbors any sort of fear, it percolates through all his thinking, makes him landlord to a ghost."

Everyone, at some time in their lives, should make time to be alone—stripped of comfort, in touch with wildness, away from noise and chatter. I have found it helpful to place myself purposely in places of clean fear. To watch the front of a thunderstorm, alone, from my front porch. To pray while perched a few feet from the edge of a mountain. To meditate after a day or so of isolated silence on the character of God. Only then, in this stunning stillness, have I realized that, in the end, we have no control.

Our children as well must be taught the fear of God. Increasingly, children are under the barrage of constant stimulation: video tapes, video games, television, CD-roms. With images coming at them at such an unheard of pace, their imagination simply crumbles under the load. And with such stunted imagination, how can they even begin to understand the fear of God? It is critical that we slow our children and expose them to deeper realities. We should teach each child to be still, for without a spirit of stillness it is impossible to hear the voice of God.

We should also attempt to teach the characteristics of God through metaphor—there are plenty in the Bible to choose from. Instead of buying your son a *Mortal Kombat II,* take him to an ocean shore and read him Psalm 77:16 ("The waters saw you, O God, the waters saw you and writhed; the very depths were convulsed."). Instead of a birthday trip to her favorite pizza place, buy your daughter a telescope and, deep into the night, wonder with her at the stars (Job 22:12 says, "Is not God in the heights of heaven? And see how lofty are the highest stars!"). Instead of watching a repeat of *Star Trek: The Next Generation,* take your children to the grave of a great-grandmother and tell them of her dreams and hopes and loves (Psalm 103:17: "As for man, his days are like grass . . . but from everlasting to everlasting the Lord's love is with those who fear him, and his righteousness with their children's children.").

The fear of the Lord is the beginning of wisdom. Unlike the world's fear, the fear of the Lord should not be harbored, resisted, or ignored. Instead, with each realization of it, we should let it cleanly pass through us, cleansing us with the correct perspective of the greatness of the danger, the smallness of our abilities, and the even greater grace, power, and love of God. When we trust God and release the danger to him, perfect love casts out fear. Then, and only then, will we hear the voice of many waters saying gently, "Do not be afraid."

❧

In July, 1964, our family took a vacation to the New York State World's Fair. There is a good deal that sticks in my mind about that fair: the state-of-the-art exhibition of talking presidents, the Johnson Wax Surround Theater, the revolving GE history of science and technology exhibit. It was there, in a blitz of the future and the promotion and promise of a better world through technology, that I was enthralled with the possibility, the motion, the compressed energy of the world. Indeed, a new and better world seemed to be on its way.

But, in the end, it was fear that made the strongest impression on me. My dad, mom, Bev, Jim, Tim, and I had been observing a demonstration of Tahitian dancers. After watching for about five minutes, Dad, Mom, Bev, and Jim turned to leave, assuming that Tim and I would automatically follow. Tim and I, however, were so enraptured by the wild beating of sticks, the frenzied precision of motion, and the color of the flames that we did not move.

About a block away from where they had left us, our family realized that we were missing. About the same time Tim and I suddenly understood that we had been separated. We were lost among thousands and thousands of people, engulfed by exhibitions of electricity, engines, and progress. We were terrified.

Tim and I tried not to panic. My father had always instructed, "If you get lost, stay right where you are; don't try to find us, I will find you." So we stood there for five to ten minutes, paralyzed, back-to-back, while the Tahitian dancers gyrated in rhythm to our fears.

And then, in the distance, we heard my father's voice and, finally, felt the security of his long arms wrap around us in love. Funny, all I could think of at the time was the release of my fear. It wasn't until years later, with children of my own, that I understood the joy of my father.

5 *INNOCENCE*

Certainly Adam in Paradise had not more sweet and curious apprehensions of the world, than I when I was a child.

THOMAS TRAHERNE ❧

When my uncle Elwood was a boy he was hit by a car. I do not know when I first became aware of this fact. Perhaps my parents told it to me as a warning of what can happen when little boys accidentally wander into the street, or maybe it simply came up in conversation like a cork rising in water, and there it was for the rest of my life—buoyant, unstoppable, problematic.

He was nine when it happened. Climbing off the back end of a truck, his arms filled with a bundle of newspapers he was to deliver, he fell off and was immediately run over feet to head. The impact knocked both of his eyes out of their sockets. His father—my grandfather—was hurriedly summoned from his job at the nearby train depot, and, arriving at the scene, asked some bystanders to go to the corner store for ice. He then calmly put his nine-year-old son's eyes back in their sockets, packed his head in the ice, and took him home.

My uncle, who was in a coma for three days, seemed to recover completely with no long-term side effects other than the fact that, once an extrovert, he became more cautious with his words, as if he might, at any given moment, get blindsided by a careless and too-active verb. He seldom said things by accident.

Uncle Elwood always fascinated me, although I probably spoke fewer words to him in my entire life than I spoke to any other of my uncles in a single day. My guess is that he was not particularly gifted at talking to children. Despite the fact that he had suffered a severe blow to the head—or (as I often wondered) maybe because of this—the man had a remarkable mind and a vocabulary that made children avoid him as surely as helium rises. "Juxtaposition" he may have said, and I was out the door looking for the nearest swing; "infiltrated" he would toss casually into a conversation, and I would escape to find out what was for supper.

Sometime after my parents had shared with me about my uncle's accident, I heard them say he was an atheist. I wasn't sure what this was, but I knew by their tone of voice that it was serious. When I asked, my parents explained to me that atheists don't believe in God.

This was a new concept for me. For one thing, I had been raised in a God-fearing, God-believing, God-in-casual-conversation home. But even beyond that, I believe the concept of God is as natural to a child raised in love as oxygen is to lungs. I had never even stopped to think about the existence of God; as far as I knew, it was never even up for debate.

What I had failed to hear about my uncle's atheism was that it was a past condition—he had been born again almost six years before I was even born the first time. Instead, for some inexplicable reason, I lived my entire childhood and much of my early adult life thinking that Uncle Elwood did not believe in God.

In an uncritical and non-sarcastic sort of way, I connected my uncle's accident with his presumed atheism. I wondered if atheism could have been a side effect to a severe blow on the head. Though I never would have admitted it to my parents, my uncle's personal atheism increased my sense of intrigue with him. Here was a person whose eyes once were out of their sockets and who did not believe in God. He possessed, for me, a kind of magnetism—he was someone from whom you never knew what to expect.

Little children see things in a unique and transitory way. I am not talking here about eye charts or toy dinosaurs spotted at unfathomable distances, but rather an uncluttered perspective that springs from simply being and allows children to remain open to the deep realities of life.

I wish I knew the best word for that child-like quality Jesus spoke of when he said, "I praise you, Father, Lord of heaven and earth, because you have hidden these things from the wise and learned, and revealed them to little children" (Matthew 11:25). Innocence, in a limited sense, is as close as I can come. Other words that hint at the reality but never fully hit the target are humility, meekness, transparency, simplicity, and openness.

I also hesitate to use the word innocence, for, in addition to its limitedness, it is also a word that can be interpreted in many ways, most of which most assuredly do not apply to little children. When my sons defiantly look me in the eye and do exactly what I just told them not to do, they are certainly not innocent. When they spit, beat on each other, take toys from church, and run in the grocery aisles, they are, from any perspective you care to look at it, not innocent. As a parent of preschoolers I could go on and on; children, for the most part, operate for selfish reasons.

Yet, at the same time, there is in their selfish pursuits, if not purity, a certain lack of guile. In this kind of innocence is embedded a naiveté or ignorance that simply does not permit children to be treacherous or apathetic. Because they cannot control the strength of the realities that hit them in their everyday world, they are left with few options but curiosity and exploration.

As a child, I remember how Tim and I used to go into my father's garage and watch him use a grindstone. I am not even sure I was aware that he was sharpening tools, but I was transfixed with the trail of orange spark. Because I did not understand the concepts of friction or combustion, I was, without dismissing the phenomenon altogether, left with no other options but to believe my father was some sort of magician.

A good deal of this kind of innocence is connected to wonder. For children, the world is new every moment and endlessly creative. Such an innocence is the womb of wonder—without any other clue, life is too large to be ignored or controlled.

But it is also more than a sense of wonder. A childlike innocence is both open to possibility and anchored in humility. The largeness of possibility—an uncle whose eyes fell out of their sockets, the questioned existence of God—is matched by a smallness, a meek and correct instinct that there is not much a child can do when faced with such realities. Wonder is only a spark that can light an open-eyed innocence. Without the environment of humility—a realization of the world and where we stand in it, a correct perspective without pride—innocence lacks the proper nutrients to grow.

We didn't see a great deal of Uncle Elwood's family because they lived two hundred miles away in Columbus. But the infrequency of our visits, rather than decreasing the memory of my uncle, strengthened it; his mystique never had a chance to fade into reality.

Part of what I liked best about Uncle Elwood was his house, which was a massive, three-story, brick home. A sense of sturdiness pervaded the place with its high ceilings, raw wood floors, and arched doorways; in these surroundings time seemed to simply pass away like a skipping stone on ice, as if, in a second, nothing had ever happened.

The second and third floors, however, held the *real* mystery and power of the house. On these floors my uncle and aunt ran a boarding house for female students who attended Ohio State University. When Tim and I were first introduced to this fact we may have been ten or eleven. Not yet under the full assault of hormones, we were just becoming aware of the intriguing difference between us—boys—and them—girls. It wasn't so much the drawings we had seen on certain, now dog-eared, pages in our Family Health Book, but the strange and instinctive pool of sparks that fell down our spines when a grown blonde wore shorts.

One Thanksgiving Day the mystery and intrigue of those two upper floors became too much for a ten-year-old. My father, whom I suspected to be brilliant, and my uncle, whom I was convinced was an atheist, had settled in the living room to watch football and were engaged in an intense conversation about the existence of God. A magic swarm of smells wafted from the kitchen, where my aunt and my mother had taken up residence.

Tim and I were drawn to the stairs that led to the second floor. Up there, our eyes said, that's where they live. College females. Each time we visited Uncle Elwood's house, our parents warned us not to go up those stairs, which, of course, served only to heighten an already overheated curiosity. What was it they did not want us to see? What harm could there be in a quick look? And most intriguing and intimidating of all, what would these college females be doing?

Tim went first. A few steps and a look into the living room. "Sanctification," my father continued. I followed Tim, carefully placing one foot after the other, one step, two steps, three steps. We both stood still, glancing again into the living room. "Immaculate conception," my uncle answered with an atheistic jeer. Clearly, my father and uncle were focused on bigger stakes than keeping track of us. And then, as fast as our hearts were racing, we were on the second floor.

I felt guilty immediately. With my dad and uncle fixed on eternal realities how could I justify not only my disobedience, but this fleshy, prickly obsession? Still, for the next ten minutes Tim and I managed to ignore a higher calling as we wandered the second floor of the house.

As the television announcer observed a fumble on the six-yard line and my uncle and my father lobbed around lofty concepts like immutability and regeneration, Tim and I were lost in a new world, wondering if we would ever be the same again. Although all of the girls had gone home for the holiday, the second floor of Uncle Elwood's house changed the way that Tim and I looked at life. We were confronted with a new reality we would face, in one manner or another, from then on: nylons, hair curlers, the feel of velvet, the light, moist scent that lingered in the empty rooms.

Upon returning downstairs, we found my uncle and my father still involved in their discussion; from my point of view, it was clear that the existence of God had not yet been settled. In any case, we had not been missed. Little did they know that Tim and I, humbly shaken, had just connected to one of life's greatest mysteries: the opposite sex. Never again would we view women through the lens of innocence.

In many ways, growing up is about learning how to shut down. As children become more independent they are less overwhelmed by the world. They no longer simply react to their environment, but act upon it with focus, control, knowledge, and skill.

Through learned skills and experience, they begin to sort through the confusing maze of options open to them and choose among the many. Instead of chasing a falling leaf in overlapping circles, a child learns to wait for it to drop. Instead of putting Legos together in a haphazard fashion, he builds a ship. Instead of sticking plastic letters under the couch, she forms a word. In doing this, the child, by his or her choice, is not only choosing one option, but, for the time being, eliminating all others.

Children move, in many ways, from simple being to purposeful doing as they learn to accept and meet new responsibilities, tasks, and duties. Along this journey to adulthood, it is inevitable that some amount of child-like innocence is lost—to remain ignorant of evil is evil. When we understand evil, we must face it. The most dangerous people I know are adult children who hide behind a facade of innocence, incapable or unwilling to accept their role as an adult in a fallen, deeply troubled world.

Innocence is also exchanged for the hope of power, security, safety or comfort. There is nothing wrong with hoping for security, safety, or comfort as long as we look at them from the perspective that they allow each of us to do the work of faith, which is to love God and love others. The problem comes when this perspective is warped by pride. For, as we become more skillful at manipulating our world, we are tempted to believe we can accomplish more than we actually can.

Instead of operating for the reason of faith expressing itself in love, we control others for our own selfish purposes. We learn quickly that fear can be reduced with a security light and that pain can be avoided by building relational walls. Seldom, until it is far too late, do any of us realize that all such attempts at personal fulfillment are illusions. We can never fully gain what we think we want. A tornado, a cancer, an argument, a divorce can smash a carefully constructed world in a second, leaving each of us ultimately helpless.

But the real disaster is not so much in what we fail to gain from trading our innocence away, but in what we lose. In order to secure personal freedom, one is forced to reduce the world to the size of an IQ, a strong will, and a high hope: things that by almost any standard by which you measure create a very small world indeed. Our existence becomes a crapshoot of to-do lists: things to avoid, things to pursue.

In such a tiny world, all the things God longs for his people to experience are reduced to less than the size of one appetite. Joy—that wide-eyed surprise of faith—becomes power or giddiness or satiation, the never-ending obsession with status and thrill. Worse yet, love is possible only when convenient. Since control must be maintained, the freedom for the kind of reckless and abandoned sort of love the Bible speaks about is torched in the flame of need. Because so much time and effort is required to meet our "responsibilities," there is very little left for fully loving God and loving others. At best, we give maybe Sunday morning, or one half hour every other morning, or maybe some money for starving children.

In such a cramped world, innocence—the uncluttered nearness to the great and transcendent realities of faith, beauty, love, God, hope—is lost in a dust cloud of quiet desperation. Eventually, all that matters is at least more than one day away—the unattainable future of those who bank on their own time and effort. And in the end, we always come up short.

❧

Innocence, I think, is most often wounded in good intentions. Think of the Pharisees. If I were reading the Gospels minus the words of Jesus, I might be fooled into believing the Pharisees were good people. They seemed harmless enough, with their white robes and chanted street-corner prayers. They were certainly filled with knowledge, and were voraciously religious and seemingly zealous for the things of God. They had good intentions, yet Jesus called them vipers.

The problem was that because of their privilege— the reserved seats at the synagogue, the admiration of the common people, the tasseled robes—the Pharisees became proud. And in their pride, they lost perspective. Refusing to recognize the proper order of reality, they reduced God and inflated themselves. Innocence, which is fueled by a largeness of awe and smallness of self, was beyond them. Their sense of wonder was reserved for a mirror; their fear was of losing position; their hope was in their own heads.

Because they were devoid of innocence, it was impossible for them to meet God at his own level. Instead, they attempted to bring him down to their own miserly world. "These things you have done and I kept silent," God complains through the Psalmist, "you thought I was altogether like you" (Psalm 50:21).

The Pharisees were not altogether unsuccessful in convincing others of their importance. In the eyes of men, they were bathed in respect, power, and authority. Yet through the eyes of Christ, we see how small they really were. Their techniques cost them a great deal. They exchanged faith for a wieldy and complex set of rules that served as boundaries and guaranteed their small, but manageable, existence. They traded in the living, dynamic, unfathomable God for a puppet god, who, with discipline and patience, could be taught to push their buttons, squirm into their rules, run in their circular wheels of need. They sacrificed wildness and grace, the transcendent, terrible, magnificent, and eternal realities of life—faith, suffering, love—for the whining, humdrum, mortal praise of men.

Internally corrupted by pride and independence, the Pharisees were stuck. Separated from innocence, fear, and humility, they were unable to see Jesus for who he was. It didn't matter that Jesus performed miracles in front of their eyes, or that they could find no error in Jesus' words— the only thing that mattered was the preservation of their carefully managed world. In the end, they resorted to murder in order to deal with Jesus' claim to be the Messiah. Innocent, the Pharisees were not.

Whether we like to believe it or not, Christians are a lot like the Pharisees; even with good intentions, we kill innocence. Often the greatest weakness we face is not from the fatigue of fighting an all-out spiritual battle but from the monotony of day-to-day living. What is holiness in the face of dozens of dirty diapers? What is salvation when the tax man comes? What is humility when your spouse makes you feel two feet tall with a cutting remark?

The loss of innocence begins when we lose sight of God in the commonplace, everyday matters of life. And when innocence finally drowns in self, as it most certainly will, then what is left is either pride or repentance. Then, as the days and months and years fall into one another, we find ourselves losing our grip on such elemental realities as wonder and fear of the Lord. We lose sight of God's order for the universe—loving God and loving others. Secretly and quite imperceptibly at first, we move to take matters into our own hands.

In church, we look for places of service, still with our eyes on heaven but with one ear tuned in for a compliment. At home, we pray for God to meet our needs and then check out the classifieds. At work, we measure our sympathy for others by proximity to the next promotion.

And, finally, when we have reduced God and others to manageable levels, we lose our innocence completely.

When this happens, as it did with the Pharisees, the level of truth shrinks to the size of one's own appetite. Instead of being an all-encompassing seizing of heart, mind and soul, Christianity is reduced to one or two singular causes—moral instruction, anti-abortion, political activism—usually designed for good intention. Yet, on close inspection, such a one-dimensional purpose statement is no longer primarily driven by the great realities of life—grace and beauty and love—but, rather, the smallish and monotonous ticking of personal need. In the end, it takes all of our effort to keep our good intentions swimming.

In order to protect our innocence, we must look at life again as children. To Tim and I, for example, something as commonplace and everyday as Uncle Elwood's house was overwhelming with its mass of oak stairs and the tender and foreign scents of college coeds' dorm rooms. In these the everyday and common places of life we were dumbstruck by the largeness of reality, forced to come to the unstoppable conclusion that life was bigger, much bigger, than two small boys in a mammoth and ancient house.

As adults, we must constantly remind ourselves of the mammoth and ancient world in which *we* find ourselves. We must, in the day-to-day movement of life, seek out the mystery, beauty, power, and wildness that constantly surround us: at church, the longing of a single voice in a song; at home, the way the light breaks and spills into a child's room; at work, the restlessness in so many discussions. Only when we begin to rediscover the magnitude of meaning in a glance or a touch or a made-up face, will we begin to see into the heart of a world where life and grace explode.

We must also seek to break from routine, for nothing dulls as much as a cycle of events and hours. Hire a babysitter and rent a Jet ski or hike a trail or make midnight love. Have family devotions in the book of Job. Fold the laundry on the front porch. Hold a staff meeting outdoors. Write a poem or belt out a song or throw a party for no reason at all.

We must do what we can to see the larger picture, to develop a constantly unsettled realization that life is beyond comprehension.

It was raining the last time I saw Uncle Elwood; not an ordinary rain, but the steady, graceless, gray rain that falls from a heavy, even sky. Gone from that ancient and sturdy house were the smells of roasting and baking and frying; gone, too, were the college girls who were on summer break, their rooms dusted and bare. What once seemed a house alive was beaten down by the unnerving and unstoppable static of silence.

At the age of fifty-four, my uncle had suffered an aneurysm and was reduced to lying in a bed in the corner of one of those massive rooms, his head bandaged and swollen badly on one side. I stood in front of him, his eyes unfocused and staring off in the distance, and all I could think of was the fact that he had been run over by a truck as a child. He would be back.

But each time we came to visit, he seemed to have slipped further away. When my dad and mom would lead me into this room I would go cold. As I searched his eyes I wondered, *Is Uncle Elwood in there? If he is, what is he thinking?* With all my heart I wanted him, even expected him, to sit up and begin an intense theological discussion with my father. When he didn't time after time after time, I had my first real cause to question the existence of God.

Years later, my father told me that, contrary to my thinking, Elwood was not an atheist. During one of the last times my father spoke to Elwood, he had asked him whether he was still believing in Jesus. Elwood, who had always been like a big brother to my father, had squeezed his hand. It may have been the last time that he communicated.

And now my parents had warned me that this might be the last time I saw him. After a few minutes of standing beside his bed, I kissed him, which I had never done before. Walking away, through my uncle's lonely room and my aunt's dormant kitchen, I found myself on the back porch. This was death, I knew, even though I had never faced it before. I cried, my tears answering the rainstorm outside.

6 *PLAY*

*The true object of all human life is play. Earth
is a task garden; heaven is a playground.*

G. K. CHESTERTON ✿

When I was two years old, my sister, Bev, the oldest of the
Wilkins siblings, was thirteen. Any astute observer will
quickly catch my point: During the most impressionable
years of my life, I was often left to the giggling, pouting,
primping, hormonally challenged mercy of a teenage girl.

I must say up front (for the sake of honesty and the
fear of retribution) that Bev was a wonderful big sister
. . . as much, that is, as such a thing is possible. She told
us stories, played endless games of Candyland with us,
and once, a few days after receiving her driving permit,
she even drove Tim, who was bleeding a few pints of
blood into the passenger seat from a newly incurred
head wound, to the doctor's office.

Yet, there was no denying that she was a teenager
(and a red-haired one at that). As hard as Bev might try,
she was constantly being flattened by the exotic and
relentless brew of hormones flowing through her brain
like fire ants at a picnic.

As proof of God's sense of humor, Bev, like many
teenagers, was completely helpless, without even a hint

of an oar in the water, at a time when she believed herself to be nearly omniscient. This rather unsettling dichotomy of fact always seemed to hover around her like a cartoon aura and made her kind of spooky.

You never knew when she was going to pop. At times, it was just an innocent little question like, "Bev, when you sit down, why do your legs get so big?" Or even a valiant, against odds effort of Tim and I to hide unnoticed behind the couch while she and her boyfriend kissed—or worse, spoke in gooey words. Could she really blame us for giggling?

All three of us brothers, even Jim (who was only four years younger than Bev), lived with a strange and agitated combination of feelings toward my sister: awe, love, fear, uncertainty, confusion, and, on the afternoon before one of her dates, nausea.

Since my mom had taken part-time work to help pay for Bev's college expenses, Bev was responsible for making supper. One time, Bev got caught up in a favorite soap opera and lost track of time—it was nearly five, and the family would be gathered around the table in less than a half hour. To make matters worse, there were no spaghetti noodles.

Jim knew instinctively what was about to happen, and, even though rain was pouring down outside, he tried to sneak out onto the roof from his bedroom window. But Bev, if not exactly playing on level ground, had more than her fair share of marbles. The next thing we knew, Tim and I were looking out the window at Jim, pulling out of the driveway on his bike, in the middle of a raging thunderstorm, pedaling as fast as he could. He looked back over his shoulder as if trying to avoid the wrath of God or the wrath of Bev—it was hard to tell which was more frightening for our big brother—and finally disappeared into the lightning-cracked distance. He was back within fifteen minutes, out of breath and mumbling something about a lightning bolt, having crossed through a mile and a half of the worst storm in recent history for a box of spaghetti noodles.

But that is not the worst of it. What we—all three of the male children—most dreaded was "the record," my sister's favorite album, Leslie Gore's *Rainbows, Sunshine and Lollipops* (or was it *Sunshine, Rainbows and Lollipops* or *Lollipops, Rainbows and Sunshine?*—just thinking of it is making me a little wacky).

If this album, whatever it was called, had been recorded a couple of decades earlier, my brothers and I were confident it would have been one of Hitler's favorite and most effective torture techniques: "Ya vont talk, eh, vell how about some Vainbows?" After two or three repetitions of "It's My Party (I'll cry if I want to, cry if I want to, cry if I want to)," even General MacArthur would have surrendered. "Let the Germans go ahead and pillage the world," we imagined him saying, "anything but *this!*"

There was something about this record that would not allow it to be played just once through. The fewest number of times I heard Bev play the album was thirty-seven times consecutively, and then she stopped it only because she had caught the kitchen on fire by forgetting she had left the bacon on high heat.

Usually somewhere about the forty-second playing, Jim, Tim, and I would decide to kill Bev. Then, we would come to our senses, realizing that Dad would probably spank us for such a terrible deed. We had to think of other alternatives, like killing Leslie Gore. Turned out, though, she had an unlisted address.

"Well, let's kill *something*," we would say to each other. And being boys, the testosterone percolating in our skulls, we would leave the house to shoot sparrows, fry an ant or two under a magnifying glass, or pour some charcoal lighter on a beetle and, with a strike of a match, make it a circus performer. (Only the Good Lord knows how many innocent birds, insects, and small rodents needlessly perished because of my sister and Leslie Gore). Whether in a sandbox, a tree house, or a patch of weeds, we found refuge, even in the worst of situations, in the perfect and instantly accessible activity of play.

In the adult world, play is considered somewhat superficial, if not harmless. It is something one does during "off" hours—a way to pass a free hour or put in some time with the kids. At best, play is looked at as a way to recharge ourselves for the important tasks of life, those things that we have to work at—a job, a marriage, a future, making the kingdom come.

There was a period of my adult life where I never watched a cloud pass in the sky, pulled the petals off a flower, skipped rocks with a friend, or challenged a twelve-year-old to a game of one-on-one. I was too busy with important issues, godly pursuits, bleeding time for another pint of possibilities. Play was welcome when it came—the toss of a Frisbee in between meetings on a planning retreat—but incomparably secondary to the work I felt I had to do.

It wasn't that I was a workaholic. Given my responsibilities and deadlines, I attempted to keep my life in balance as well as I could. I made to-do lists, sorted my priorities, and managed my time.

But in the very structuring of my life, I lost my invaluable ability to play. It is precisely when time becomes "manageable," like a circus elephant facing a whip, that the spirit of play becomes chained to the ticking of seconds. Imagine a tourist who, even before he arrives in a city, maps out a detailed route for his visit, highlighting precise streets and sites. Next to the map, he marks the time he plans to spend getting to and from and staying at the sites. What kind of vacation could this be? What if, somewhere on his way from site four to site five he encounters a man on a bench feeding pigeons, or a park full of begonias, or someone sketching a half-smiling child in charcoal?

Play can never be managed or planned, for at its core is eloquent surprise. It is, in more than one sense, the unexpected act of taking life by the throat, shaking it with irony and lightheartedness, and stepping back to listen to a moment split into bright laughter and contagious joyfulness.

It never ceases to amaze me that play, while considered of secondary importance to adults, almost never loses its attractiveness, even for the most busy and focused people. Why is it that we prefer squirrels over snakes, or stop to watch children flying kites, or stick our feet into a pool? In playfulness, there is a stubborn and tender contrast to the other realities of the world. In a fallen, decaying, sin-damaged world, the curiosity and laughter in play reminds us of something beyond the obvious, of something tinged with hope, of something as surprising and real as God himself.

But the attractiveness of play goes even deeper than that. Play, if it is nothing else, is the most immediate and recognizable bridge between being and doing. It depends upon a certain quality of being connected to things outside of oneself—the wonder, wildness, and movement of the world—and, like a child, simply reacting to these things by doing, playing, and being joy-filled.

I learned a great deal about play from our family dog, Tuffer, who joined the family when I was seven and Tim was eight. My parents, under the pretense of a family outing for a drive in the car, took us thirty miles away to Lima, to the brood full of squirming, yipping, not yapping, puppies. There were three females and one male and, to my way of thinking, no real way to choose. I wanted them all.

Tim, however, took one look at the little male dog, with a spot on the top of his head, and said softly and quite distinctly, "Daddy, get me *that* dog." My father, who has always known a good buy when he saw one, paid fifty-five dollars and, in that one moment, bought a lifetime worth of memories.

For those of you unfamiliar with the breed of Boston Terrier, imagine a standard terrier with a nose flattened as if it had run into a steam shovel. Add to that a gentle and stubborn temperament, like a slightly underfed beagle, and you have the Boston Terrier.

I think, as all dog owners must think, that Tuffer was one in a million. He was born to play. In my childhood world, there was not a place too high or too wet or too cold or too mean or too frightening he would not go.

In the swimming pool, Tuffer, waiting on my count-down, would dive in on cue. "5–4–3–2–1, go get 'em!" and he would be gone, lapping the water with his tongue as he paddled. When we threw a plastic ball with holes in it into the water, Tuffer would dive beneath the water on command, bug-eyed, and retrieve the sub-merged ball.

At Benroth's pond, a body of water just big enough to water ski on, Tuffer had a chance to display his many other aquatic abilities. He would stand on an inner tube, yap like a lunatic, and bite the tube. He also learned, on the first try, how to ride a surfboard behind our family's speed-boat. He loved the motion and would snap his jaws at the spray the board created. Needless to say, a Boston terrier on a surfboard turned more than a head or two.

Tuffer was also an avid fisherman. About three quarters of a mile from our home was a tributary stream that eventually emptied into Van Buren State Park. On many spring and summer mornings, Tim and I would pack our fishing poles, a couple of bologna sandwiches, and Tuffer onto our bicycles (Tuffer rode in a customized padded basket that fit onto the front handlebars) and pedal as fast as we could toward the stream, Tuffer's body alert and pointed like an expensive and ridiculous hood ornament.

The stream, during certain times of the year, was alive with bluegill and catfish, big enough at least to pull a bobber under water. Tuffer would sit, eyes moving between fisherman and bobber, waiting for even the smallest hint of movement. Once the bobber started to dance, he would begin to whine, under his breath almost, as if not to spook the fish.

Once the bobber was under, he would begin barking, running wildly between fisherman and the edge of the stream with the same kind of herky-jerky intensity of a coach on the sidelines. As the fish would surface, he would wade into the water, often landing the catch with his mouth.

Tuffer could not handle failure when fishing. When one would get away, he would wade deeper and deeper into the water, finally sticking his head in to see if there was any way to fix the incompetence of his two inept masters.

Once, much to the surprise of us all, I hooked into a giant catfish, nearly twenty inches long (no, make that twenty-four inches ... on second thought, thirty inches). I was only seven at the time, and small, and I think the catfish weighed nearly as much as I did. As the adventure was unfolding, two things became quickly evident to Tuffer: (1) I had hooked into a shark; (2) I was, by myself, incapable of reeling it in. Suddenly, his eyes, like a platoon leader under attack, took on a fierce, steady fire; he knew that if this monster was to be landed, it was up to him. He dove into the water, swam about four feet out, and then disappeared. Surfacing about ten seconds later, he had the catfish in his mouth, which he deposited at my feet. It didn't matter that he had been horned by the beast and was now bleeding at his lip; the victory was clearly his.

Despite his prowess in the water, land sports caused Tuffer some problems, especially football. First, there was the matter of the ball—large, oblong, and capable of causing pain. Then, too, the primary action was in knocking one another down. How was a twenty-three-pound, one-foot-six-inch dog supposed to tackle fourth- or fifth-grade boys?

Again, with imagination and perseverance, Tuffer found the solutions. The ball, he learned, would fit neatly into his jaw if he grabbed it carefully at one end (all of our footballs had teeth marks at both of the pointed ends). After much practice, Tuffer could, in fact, dance gracefully between any number of flying bodies of boys, delaying the game indefinitely.

He also discovered an ingenious method of tackling. By grabbing at the bottom of a pant leg and holding on for dear life, Tuffer could often bring down even the most bullish of boys. To this day, I still have an image in my mind of one of my friends, who would later become a star halfback during high school, headed toward our backyard goal line with Tuffer hanging from his pant leg, running the way you might if you had stepped into a bucket. It was, from any perspective, a picture of Tuffer's sheer determination.

No matter how the odds were stacked against Tuffer, he continued on in his play, for, to him, the option of being left out was simply unthinkable. Once, as the family was headed for a bike ride, my mother decided, because of the heat, that Tuffer should stay home instead of riding in his custom-designed basket. Tuffer did not take kindly to the idea; when we returned, we found several of my mother's possessions—a half-finished afghan, her slippers, some women's magazines, her bathrobe— all lying in the middle of the living room floor, each with just enough chew marks to remind my mother of her unpardonable offense. He was a dog with a highly defined and focused sense of justice.

My mother had actually been the one to name him Tuffer when we picked him out at the kennel. When she had first looked in his eyes, she caught a hint of defiance or playfulness and said to us, "What a little Tuffer!" She was right. When it came to what dogs should do best, Tuffer refused to budge on his God-given mandate of play.

Maybe it wasn't just the act of playing that Tuffer loved so much, although it certainly fed his needs for stimulation, adrenaline and proving himself equal to, or better than, all the boys of the world. When the nine boys playing ball took a halftime break for a drink of lemonade, Tuffer would sit on the porch steps, just like the rest of them, accepting an occasional pat on the head. Or on a warm and windy summer day near the home plate of our backyard baseball field, having just accomplished another win for the Detroit Tigers, we would sit side-by-side, just the two of us, silent, leaning into a summer breeze, feeling the play on our senses.

To watch someone play is, in many ways, to see deep inside them. There are some who play too timidly or too boldly, as if the act of playing is something foreign to them. For such people, play is something they must or should do; it resembles a backward child or an uptight adult, too scared or too tense to get beyond the score.

Beth is an example. She hides near the sidelines, boundaries, or foul lines. She fears play in the same nerve-splitting manner as a person who can't swim fears the water—she simply doesn't know how. At the age of twelve, her mother died and she, being the oldest sister, was forced from the playground into the kitchen. At a young age, she was overwhelmed with responsibility. Play was as distant and imaginary as a dragon in Scotland.

Greg, on the other extreme, steps into the center of play as if his life depends on it. He spikes and dives and strategizes and rips and tears at play as if it can only yield its purposes in tiny, stripped-down pieces. As the child of a workaholic father, Greg was taught, in both conscious and subtle ways, that what mattered most in life was achievement. At a young age, he was charmed by responsibility. Play was a conquest if anything at all.

Both Beth and Greg, the playground reveals, are damaged people. Play, for them, is not a matter of simplicity, for simplicity is not a reality in their lives. They see life in terms of survival or conquest; play demands work.

And then there are some who play too frequently, with a kind of recklessness that confuses simplicity with purpose. They assume that all of life is a game. Play, for such people, is an endless number of escape hatches, a running away from responsibility, blood, and pain.

Paul had a mother who gave in to all his playful whims. Because he received the toys of his choice, he did not need to develop his imagination. Instead, he played with battery-powered cars, computer-precise invaders, and emotions. Spoiled and mindless, he grew up believing play was at the measured center of everything.

It is not necessary to see Paul on a playground, for he is always there. Mistaking play for the heart of reality, he casually bleeds life of responsibility, and, with each new birthday, refuses to grow up. He skips from job to job, hungry for entertainment and diversity, and over the years, ends up poisoned, alone, the most unplayful of people.

How then *should* we play? Is it reasonable to even ask the question, or, in asking it, do we—through our adult linear thinking—destroy the multilayered dimensions of the answer? Isn't a serious consideration of play like describing green as a color?

Maybe this is why the Bible so seldom speaks of the concept of play. In the New International Version, the word "play" occurs only thirteen times, the majority of those referring to musical instruments. How is it that the Bible can virtually ignore one of the most basic and instinctive human activities? By contrast, work, which we often think of as an antonym of play, is mentioned 370 times.

Even more fascinating is the mention of work before the fall. Genesis 2:15 states, "The LORD God took the man and put him in the Garden of Eden to work it and take care of it." How could this be work in the traditional sense? What was there to do? As far as we know, there were no weeds or vicious animals or worms in the apples (with maybe one notable exception). God, who walked with Adam and Eve, graciously provided for every need. Adam and Eve, as far as I can tell, mostly walked around praising God, watching fruit spring to life, and naming the animals. Does this kind of work not sound like play? Like joy?

And even in a world of thistles and violence and death, the likes of which Christ suffered on the cross to purchase our redemption, should not the most serious and profound of a Christian's work be saturated with a spirit of play? Or should we, in the shedding of his blood, define red simply as a color?

Unfortunately, some of the most unplayful people I have met are Christians. They see play negatively from at least two perspectives. The first is what I refer to as the self-induced martyr complex. For these Christians, the world belongs to Satan, and all enjoyment, including play, is to be avoided. The second perspective is what might be called the "We-have-to-save-the-world" perspective. "When there are people dying and going to hell, how can we possibly 'waste' time with play?" some Christians may ask. To them, all of eternity precariously hangs in the balance.

Both of these perspectives are valid, biblical points of view. Yet, what they miss is a balanced view of the Christian life. Christianity stripped of an essential playfulness is a hollow, almost gutted faith. Living in such a dire urgency, we're back to the old "doing versus being"—the quantity of doing overwhelms the quality of being, and soon actions spring from a dry well of a humorless, empty soul. We have all seen such Christians—preaching judgment, demanding change, implementing plans, offensively defensive, and every bit as playful as a one-legged mother hen. What kind of a witness is that?

In such a state, Christians risk the possibility of becoming less than beasts, for often we come to believe, given the press of evil and the lack of joy we experience, that *we* have to make things happen. Change becomes a matter of how hard we work, how much we do.

To me, play seems to be critical to the human spirit for at least three reasons. First, it springs from an unconscious sense of celebration. The beasts, like Tuffer and Cocoa, are naturally given to play.

My brothers and sister rode No. 7, the oldest of all of Van Buren's school buses. We were the last ones off the bus; by a quirk of planning, we passed our house as we headed south on Old Dixie Highway, but were forced to stay on the bus until it returned, heading north.

On the first pass of bus No. 7, we could always look out the bus window and see Tuffer and Cocoa watching for us. At precisely 3:15 every weekday afternoon, they would stop whatever they were doing—usually sleeping in the sun or eating—and head toward our front yard, where they would, side by side, sit and stand. When the bus would pass, Tuffer would start to shake; Cocoa would whinny. When we finally arrived ten minutes or so later, there they were, dog and pony, to welcome us once again to our world of play.

Tuffer and Cocoa, of course, were beasts who had no bills to pay or future suppers to worry over. What else were they going to do—write scripts for a Broadway play or study metaphysics? Their lives, stripped of the necessity of survival and absent of any overriding purpose, were abandoned to play.

Psalm 104 speaks of God and praises brute beasts:

He makes springs pour water into the ravines;
  it flows between the mountains.
They give water to all the beasts of the field;
  the wild donkeys quench their thirst.
The birds of the air nest by the waters;
  they sing among the branches.
He waters the mountains from his upper chambers;
  the earth is satisfied by the fruit of his work.
He makes grass grow for the cattle.

The verbs in this poem are interesting. In *connection* with God's actions, they are related to giving—"pour," "give," "waters," "makes." And in *response* to God's actions, the beasts "quench," "nest," "sing," and "are satisfied." There is, in each of these "response" verbs, a sense of freedom, a certain room for playfulness, worship, and joy. They know, without thinking about it, what they were created for.

To humans as well, play is the conscious recognition of God's life-giving nature. In Psalm 104, man is also addressed:

> [God makes] plants for man to cultivate—
> bringing forth food from the earth:
> wine that gladdens the heart of man,
>   oil to make his face shine,
>   and bread that sustains his heart.

Again, the word choices sparkle with a sense of freedom: "gladdens," "shine," "sustains." The same promises of shelter, food and joy are repeated throughout the New Testament for those who have faith.

Play is also important for another reason. Through it, relationships form and deepen. In your own life, how many of your friendships have developed through play? Because it is one of the most basic and unencumbered of human activities, play often helps us to relate to others in ways we possibly could not otherwise.

In addition to cultivating a correct *perspective* about play, we must also just do it. We must deliberately set aside time for play in all facets of our lives— as spouse, father, worker, friend, child of God. Picnics should be planned, date nights set, children regularly tackled and tickled.

But, most importantly, a sense of play should be an attitude that is very near the center of who we are, not just in set aside and spontaneous moments, but at all times. Play is a high form of worship. It says to the world that

God is in control, that gifts are his to give, and that we receive them with great joy. Although there is still much to be done (man *is* responsible for *joining* God in his work), it is clear that the work of cultivating and bringing forth of Psalm 104 is ripe with joy, trust, and worship.

In such an environment of glad hearts, shining faces, and sustained hearts, is play surprising? Can the voice help but dance, the feet keep from skipping, and even the hardest of hearts resist the shouts of praise?

All this is not to say that the work is easy. Faith in God involves perseverance, suffering, and fortitude. There are, for sure, the Leslie Gores of the world singing, over and over again, "It's my party, It's my party," driving conscientious Christians to the verge of retching. But it is then, and maybe most especially then, that we know that we dance to a higher and more playful tune.

7 IMAGINATION

The Possible's slow fuse is lit by the imagination.

EMILY DICKINSON ❧

Tim and I grew up when nearly the whole world was shooting for the moon.

There was, in fact, never a time in my childhood when space, that great black otherness, wasn't within reach. I was four and Tim was five when Alan Shepherd, in that sardine-like can called Freedom 7, was the first American launched into suborbital space. A year later, in Friendship 7, John Glenn, with all of his right stuff, was the first American to orbit the earth.

The heart of our childhood was, in one way or another, marked by the penetration of space, the conquest of distance, and the realization of the impossible: man on the moon. It was more than just the riddle of the unknown, the power of the rockets, the gutsy earthiness of names like Gus and Buzz and Butch, the spiky adrenaline of the letters USSR, or even the first chalky, surreal step on the moon—it was the dark piercing of heaven itself. It was a rare time, a time when the wildest of imaginations became reality.

I can remember sitting with Tim in front of the Motorola combination hi-fi and black-and-white television watching the progression of NASA missions—Mercury to Gemini to Apollo—finding ourselves transfixed with possibility and danger. We watched Edward White "walk" in space during Gemini IV, and then, tragically, burn along with Gus Grissom and Roger Chaffee in a ground fire of Apollo 1; we held our breath as Apollo 8, the first flight out of earth's orbit, sent back pictures of the moon; and, of course, we were amazed with Apollo 11—man's first step on the moon and the words that seemed to cross the unfathomable chasm between impossibility and actuality: "That's one small step for man; one giant leap for mankind."

Perhaps most vividly of all, I remember the ill-fated Apollo 13. Curiously, I had just turned thirteen myself. I remember wandering into our backyard, my head just beginning to reel with the rush of hormones, and looking up into a cool, crisp night, lit by a full moon. I tried to pray, I think, but my mind wandered to the realities of powerlessness, the notion of being stranded in the depths of space, illuminated in unearthly bright white, like ghosts, and falling into the hand of God. Who, I wondered, would hear their screams?

As space exploration unraveled before us, Tim and I, with blankets and cardboard and enough Tang to color anyone's dreams, also launched ourselves into the stratosphere.

We skipped most of the Mercury program, partially on account of the fact we were still trying to master our bladders let alone the deep mysteries of space, but mostly because there were two of us, and Tim, who felt an urgent calling to be Commander, needed someone to command. One, in the deep, lonely void of that kind of space (or, in our case, the basement), was simply the wrong number.

In addition to being older, the commander, and the pilot, Tim was also the architect of our imaginations. He had a knack for technical details (or, pretended quite convincingly he did), and he was the one to design and engineer the exterior and interior of our spacecrafts.

He would begin with the skeleton of the craft—mainly chairs, but also lamps and poles and even fireplace pokers—all arranged with their backs facing into what would be the interior of the spaceship. He would then, carefully and with little or no regard to color coordination, spread as many blankets and rugs and sheets as necessary, which was usually barely adequate to cover the craft, but more than enough to bring my father, cool in front of a televised football game, into the room to reclaim an afghan.

My job was to, upon command, assist in the placing of the blankets—which I rarely did right—and to, if necessary, steal into the living room, wait for my father to go to sleep, and take back the afghan. Tim would assure me that Dad would simply have to make sacrifices for such a worthy cause as the exploration of deep space. This, I might add, was fine for him to say, because he—as he was always quick to point out to my father—was not the one who took his blanket.

After the exterior was complete, Tim would focus his attention on the interior. On pieces of cardboard, he would draw endless gauges and dials and switches, in scientific shades of purple and rust orange and burgundy (apparently *real* astronauts were not fond of bright, primary colors). He would then put together the remaining necessities of space flight—buckets of Tang; dry bologna sandwiches; space manuals and logs; the lightbulb from a microscope; sometimes Tuffer (when Tim felt like putting up with his endless requests for space walks to go pee); football helmets covered with plastic, with just enough punched out holes to breath; ink pens; a Texas Instruments calculator; antiperspirant; and, much to my brother's chagrin, a couple of my favorite Dr. Seuss books (I found *The Cat in the Hat* especially comforting when we were stranded in space just before bedtime).

Our missions became quite elaborate and sophisticated. When he discovered Dad's tool chest, Tim's imagination knew no bounds. Instead of the primitively drawn dials and switches and controls, Tim began to use the real things, each stuck, at first, strategically through cardboard and, later, tacked and nailed into wood. Once, in a stroke of pure engineering genius, Tim hooked up some switches and tiny lights to a 6-volt, industrial lantern battery, and, for three or four orbits of the earth, we had the most impressive looking control panel known to childhood. Soon thereafter however, one of my Dr. Seuss books—*Green Eggs and Ham,* I think—caught fire, and we had to abort the entire mission after Tuffer, quite alarmed, ripped a hole in the side of the spacecraft, blankets trailing in his panicked wake.

But it was our imaginations, mostly, that soared. Instead of being grounded in the basement amid a collection of furniture, blankets, cardboard, and crayons, we launched ourselves into deep space, thousand of miles and another dimension away. Instead of the smell of crackers, sweat, and dog breath, we breathed in the unmistakable stench of nothingness, the clean aroma of dehydrated water. Instead of pajamas with bunny feet, space suits. Instead of a trip to the bathroom, a tethered walk in space. Instead of a gray, November afternoon on earth, a white-silver moon or the blue-green jewel of a planet.

"Imagination," writes author Ursula Le Guin, "makes me human and makes me a fool; it gives me all the world and exiles me from it." Is this not the picture of a child, living in imaginary worlds, yet eventually forced to grow up in the "real" one?

As a child, especially during summers away from arithmetic and penmanship, I lived in my imagination. Many hot and breezy afternoons were spent in a pennant race as a shortstop for the Detroit Tigers, batting an unheard of .473, with best friends right fielder Jim Northrup and pitcher Mickey Lolich.

In a side yard of my childhood home stood a garage with a sloping roof. I would stand about fifty yards away with a plastic bat wrapped at the sweet spot with electrical tape, and would toss one of my brother Jim's used tennis balls up in the air and hit it. If the ball landed short of the garage, it was an automatic out; if the ball hit the concrete wall on the bounce, it was a single (and here Tuffer, who was always my fielder and retriever, would often steal hits with his graceful prowess); if it hit the roof, it was a double; if it found a small space between the end of a garage and a nearby tree, it was a triple; and, of course, if the ball sailed over the roof, it was a homer.

Barring a trip to an amusement park or a few too many of my mother's chocolate cupcakes, Tuffer and I would be out in our side yard, the home of the Detroit Tigers, day after day, hour after hour, batter by batter, swing after swing. We would play a full season straight through, except on days when the sun was hot and flat, and Tuffer, about the seventh inning of the second game, with the ball in his mouth, would run for the swimming pool and take a few laps before returning.

In addition to playing the game, I would score it. Dick McCauliffe, 2B, a single in the third; a strikeout in the fourth; safe on an error in the seventh; and an RBI double in the ninth. Final tally: 4 2 2 1, bringing his batting average to .312.

The pitchers, too, were meticulously charted for each game—number of strikeouts, walks, hits, earned runs, as well as accumulative numbers: ERA, walk/strikeout ratio, and, of course, wins and losses. In my 1965 side yard season, Mickey Lolich ended up with a 37–1 record (he had the flu on the day of his only loss) with a 0.72 ERA. That record was bested only by an upstart young pitcher, who, when he wasn't pitching, played shortstop: I was 40–0, with a 0.37 ERA (my only weakness an inexplicable tendency to give up homers to Boog Powell, the Baltimore Orioles' massive first baseman).

Such were the foolish days of my childhood summers. With the change of seasons, of course, came a change of uniform. With the advent of fall, I would don my Sears & Roebuck football uniform, with its durable pressed cardboard thigh protectors, put on my helmet (rescued from outer space and all remnants of plastic wrap), and pretend that my #21 jersey was actually a #22, and I was Bullet Bob Hayes, the fastest man on earth and wide receiver for the Dallas Cowboys.

Basketball season was conducted in a concrete room of the basement that was rarely visited by other family members. Masking tape held the season together: a coat hanger rim heavily taped to the wall, a net carefully strung with string and taped to the rim, and, in much the manner of paint (which Dad had firmly forbid), tape also marked foul line, the lane, half court line and circle. Later, masking tape in the form of a large #21 honored the game's most graceful and grace-filled player. (I couldn't find a #22 in a basketball uniform either.) One season I averaged, if I remember right, 73.8 points a game.

Imagination is a bridge between the heart and mind, the seen and the unseen, science and art, the actual and the possible, law and grace, willingness and will, reason and emotion, chaos and order, the verifiable and the transcendent. All that matters, in one way or another, is bridged through imagination.

By taking the raw material of experience and intu-ition, imagination reshapes the world through hopes and dreams. If ever there was an argument against Dar-win, it is the existence of imagination. If survival of the fittest is all that matters, there would be no reason for humans to "evolve" imagination.

Author Henry Miller wrote that "imagination is the voice of daring; if there is anything Godlike about God it is that; he dared to imagine everything." Given this, it is not surprising, given a summer's afternoon and a proper size patch of green grass, that a child will dare to imagine a major league deal. Or given a Dixie cup, some string and glue, that he or she will create a dock-ing in space. Or that a pile of sand bordered by one by eights becomes an entirely new world. A child, who has yet to learn that not everything is possible, will be dar-ing in his imagination.

In a fallen world, imagination is both dangerous and necessary—dangerous because, like all other God-imaged characteristics, it could be used to advance the cause of self; necessary because, without it, there would be no way to realize even the possibility of redemption.

In my childhood imagination, more times than not, I was the center of my creation. I had a batting average of .473, a scoring average of 73.8, and a sandbox world named in my honor. This, of course, was fantasy, twisted to shape the image of a little boy.

But even though such imagination is perverted by the push of self, there is in it something invaluable: the daring intuition that anything is possible. "Out of nothing," the Bible tells us, "God created everything that is."

As we move from child to adult, from the colors of a kaleidoscope to the black-and-white of arithmetic, we run the danger of diluting the imagination. Facts, if we are not careful, will become more important than the truth behind the facts. Physics, if we are not on our toes, will reduce us into believing that the sun is no more than a collection of burning gases. And music, if we do not have an ear to hear, will become nothing more than notes and octaves and chords.

In such a stilted, concrete world of facts, the temptation is to reduce the world to law. Boundaries can be defined, experiments verified, objects consistently manipulated, theories put forth, the weather predicted, and, without even knowing it, we come to the startling, false conclusion that control is possible.

Science, in this sense, is dangerous. In its effort to explain, science always reduces, always tears apart. All that cannot be reduced or studied is simply dismissed. Imagination, on the other hand, is never content with mere explanation. In an effort to transform, imagination always expands, connects, and brings together. Like a curious and energetic circus clown, imagination moves in and out of different dimensions, spinning a plate here, dropping a joke there, testing a rope here, and then, only then, delivering a punch line.

This is not to say that there is, or should be, no connection between facts and reality. Yet, because the world is teeming with the transcendent, the supernatural, and the invisible—those stubborn phenomena that refuse to be reduced or studied—it is the daring work and clever play of the imagination to expand those facts into truth.

Without imagination, the experience of being human is also reduced. Sex becomes a matter of hormones; willpower is helpless against imprinted genes; reason is nothing more than a loose collection of facts; and love, that most mysterious and complex outreach of mind and soul, is simply unthinkable.

John is a man who, when he won an Eagle Scout award at the age of fourteen, knot by knot, let go of imagination. All of his life, he has worked diligently and efficiently, with maximum results. Through his hard work, he has won awards, earned money and respect, and even led a sinner or two toward redemption. He is a man committed to commitment, dedication, perseverance, and responsibility. The problem is, he is dead. He has, in his efficiency and self- sufficiency, lost the ability to imagine a wild and unfettered relationship, one impossible to direct much less control, and he often confuses the chaos that is love as something to avoid.

Chandra is a run down woman with no energy trapped in a tiny world of diapers, dishes, fighting children, and a husband hiding behind his responsibilities. Menaced by Oprah, and other women of *purpose*, she feels unappreciated, lonely, wasted. She has lost the ability to imagine that the vital actions of life are found in the day-to-day routine of wiping up drool, soothing of spirits, and giving instructions.

Sheila is frustrated. Occasionally sparked by the Holy Spirit, she remembers her past failed attempts at doing good, of making a difference. Like a woman staring at a wall slick with Vaseline, she sees only the desperate marks left by her slipping fingers. She is too tired, she says, to try again. In her active and bitter struggle with sin, she has difficulty imagining the outrageous nature of grace.

In these, and in all of us with wounded imaginations, lie the tortured landscape of winter, the yellows and grays and browns of February—the hopeless facts. And yet we long for something more.

Imagine a planet, one of nine, let's say, the fourth in orbit around a sun. A silver-blue jewel against the blackness of space with an atmosphere consisting of seventy-eight percent nitrogen and twenty-one percent oxygen, suspended in space by who knows what. Revolving around the sun at the speed of 18.5 miles per second, it is a tiny speck of matter no more than 8,000 miles in diameter. In the overall scheme of things, it is a picture of insignificance, lost in the magnitude of a cold, silent void.

Imagine a sun, just one among the one hundred fifty billion stars traveling around the center of this galaxy. With temperatures soaring to twenty-five million degrees Fahrenheit, its hydrogen is converted into helium, releasing enormous amounts of energy, the most abundant and curious being a radiation known as light.

Imagine a solar system, a collection of debris caught by the sun's gravity in relentless orbits—asteroids, meteors, comets, gas, satellites and planets. All, in the terminology of the cosmos, relatively jammed together in the space of a few billion miles.

Imagine a small galaxy, spherical in shape, consisting of a mere one hundred fifty billion or so stars, with a diameter of five hundred thousand light years. Just one galaxy among an infinity of endless galaxies.

And if, by a superhuman stretch of the imagination, you have managed to paint a mental picture, you still have only a minuscule hint of God—just one brush stroke from a one-haired brush on a postage-stamp canvas against the backdrop of eternity.

There is simply no way to imagine God. He is larger than the cosmos, more endless than eternity, more powerful than a billion stars, frenetic, creative, volatile, inherently supernatural. He is in control, sustaining, immovable, unflinching, a voice deeper and blacker than the drumming silence of the cosmos—a God whose touch has the bite of an exploding sun, whose single breath is likely to stretch from Ursa Major to Capricorn, to say nothing of the power and range of his holiness.

And in the universe unleashed through his words, in one of the smaller constellations, in a rather common galaxy, in a tiny solar system, on the fourth planet in orbit around one of the one hundred fifty billion stars, in a tiny, sand-brushed village called Bethlehem, in an animal manger, lying in a feeding trough still reeking of saliva, imagine this same God, crying and helpless.

Into time and space and flesh and bone—laid low by love—he became man.

Who can imagine God as a puny creature, skin and bones, yards of intestines and capillaries, bound to time and place? God as man to suffer with and for man.

Imagine the cross. To trees he had grown, his flesh was nailed. By the people he had created and loved, the nails were hammered. For the sins he so despised, he suffered. From the pinnacle of praise and life, he descended into death. For those who deserved hell, his death gave the possibility of heaven.

What is the cross, but the undiluted imaginative and outrageous love of God? Christ came, the Bible tells us, so that we might have life, and have it more abundantly. The freedom of the cross is the promise of salvation secured and death overcome.

Yet we are reminded that we live in an unimaginative world, with people of unimaginative faith, if they have any at all. At best, we are busy with life and focused on the urgent press of self in a world that just doesn't seem to care. At worst, we are incapable of seeing past the black-and-white demands of the law, stuck in facts, living our lives chained to a buzzsaw of approval.

As Christians freed from the judgment of sin, we have no need to secure a redemption already won. Loved unconditionally, there is no need to primp and patter after the approval of others. Provided for as a child of God, we have been given the promises of shelter, food, and whatever is necessary. We have been given the freedom to be ourselves, to love, to respond imaginatively to the outrageous love of God.

The problem is that the Christian community suffers from an atrophy of the imagination. We have been led into the mistaken notion that the more facts we know about God, the better Christians we'll be. The fact is, there are some mysteries in life—the cross, the magnitude of grace, the wild passion and love of God for his people—that simply cannot be understood through reason alone. Although not disconnected from reason, they are on a higher plane than mere intellectual thought. "For my thoughts are not your thoughts," God says to us in Isaiah, "neither are your ways my ways" (Isaiah 55:8).

The only way we can come to grips with realities such as these is through the imagination. I love what Wendell Berry writes in his book, *Standing by Words*: "The imagination is our way into the divine Imagination, permitting us to see wholly—as whole and holy—what we perceive as scattered, as order what we perceive as random." Imagination involves all of who we are—both the mind and the emotion—in transforming thoughts or words into images or voices or visions.

As a community of believers it is vital that we recover our imagination. When imagination is lost, life-giving wisdom degenerates into lifeless facts, soaring grace is grounded once again in the dung heap of the law, and we live in prisons of fear, disappointment, anger, busyness, and resentment.

To stretch your imagination you may find it helpful to study a particular theological concept, not just through word studies, but by reflecting on metaphors. Take grace (or forgiveness), for example. Because the idea is so far beyond human reason, the Bible makes frequent use of metaphor in an attempt to engage our imagination. "For as high as the heavens are above the earth, so great is his love for those who fear him; as far as the east is from the west, so far has he removed our transgressions from us. As a father has compassion on his children, so the LORD has compassion on his children" (Psalm 103:11–13). Here, three powerful metaphors are employed—the height of the heavens, the distance between east and west, and the love of a father for a child—to *involve* us in the grace, love, and forgiveness of God.

Clearly, the purpose of presenting such metaphors is not so they will be broken down and parsed but, quite the opposite, so that they will connect us—from one image to the next—to a new perception. I am not saying that analytical study is not important, but I do believe biblical language is often designed to jump start our senses—our hearing, touching, seeing—in a way that cannot be realized only through our intellect. Concepts such as grace may very well never have their full impact upon us until our imaginations are reactivated.

Let us return to the idea of grace—see, hear, and feel the power of metaphor.

The snow began in the mid-morning hours, falling softly and patiently into the morning sun like flakes of fire. Unlike most winter storms in northern Ohio, which bruised and pelted and surged, this snowfall was quiet, heavy, inexpressibly neutral. It continued throughout the day and into the cool distance of the evening, muffling words and a world full of colors beneath an endless, smooth blanket of white.

I was barely nine, just beginning to seriously toy with arithmetic, and here was a winter's day beyond anyone's wildest calculations. I stood in the front yard of my childhood home and wondered where the world had gone. Everything, it seemed to me, was transformed—the yellow-browns of winter, the distance, my voice tossed to the sky—and what was left was not only different, but charged. Unseen forces were at work—in such a snowfall, the power of imagination, the work of grace.

That same sense of the unseen stays with us today. "Come," says the Lord, "let us reason together—your sins, though blood-red, will be washed white as snow." Into our February landscapes, softly descends the possibility, white as snow, white as snow, white as snow . . .

8 *FAITH*

Faith is the highest passion in a human being. Many in every generation may not come that far, but none comes farther.

OLIVER WENDELL HOLMES ✺

When my oldest son, Taylor, was just a little more than three, he became fascinated with heaven. It started, as it usually does with children, innocently enough, when an adult was talking about our neighbor, an elderly man, who was about to have serious surgery. "Jesus may take Joe to heaven," was what someone said in Taylor's presence. At the time, he asked no questions.

A few days later, however, Taylor came screaming and running from our backyard, which borders Joe's house. "Daddy, Daddy," he screamed, as terrified as I had ever seen him. I hugged him and tried to calm him. "Daddy, don't let"—and he lost his words in another sob—"don't let Jesus come and take me to heaven." He cried for a long time as I wrapped him tightly in my arms. "I want to stay with you and Mommy. Please don't let Jesus get me."

I did not know what to say. How can you assure a child about heaven without making Jesus out to be a thief in the night?

"I think it will probably be a long time before Jesus comes to take you to heaven," I assured him.

"After Halloween?" Taylor inquired.

"A long time after Halloween."

"But not lasterday [yesterday]?"

I could see I needed to change my approach. I felt myself grasping for straws.

"Sometimes old people like Joe die," I tried to explain. "Their bodies just get old and tired, and they don't feel so good, and pretty soon their bodies just stop working. But you don't have to worry, you're not old at all; you're only three."

"But, Dad, you're kinda old."

"You're kinda right, Taylor," I said, laughing.

"Is Jesus going to come and take you to heaven cause you're kinda old?" Taylor continued.

"I don't think so," I replied. "I'll stick around so you still have someone to play sea monster with. Mommy doesn't make a very good sea monster; she's too nice."

"But Mommy sings pretty. Does Mommy sing pretty, Daddy?"

"Yeah, honey, Mommy sings real pretty."

Taylor had finally settled, and he sat quietly; I could see our words, like so many gummy worms, being digested. After a minute or two, the conversation continued.

"Daddy, what's heaven?"

"Uh . . . uhm . . . uh."

"Well," said Taylor, with a scrunched-up nose that meant determination, "I don't want to go to heaven, not ever. Jesus can't come and get me. I won't let him."

"Oh, honey, but heaven is a nice place. It's like one big, huge, gigantic sandbox. You'd really like it."

This brought up a few new points of interest. "Does Jesus have a 'dozer?"

"Bigger than our whole house."

"How 'bout buckets?"

"Big as a swimming pool . . ." I said solemnly.

"But Jesus willn't throw sand at other pepple [people], will he?"

"No, sweetie, Jesus doesn't throw sand at other people because that's bad, and Jesus does only good things," and here, taking advantage of every opportunity, I added, with special emphasis, "*just like big boys should do only good things.*"

"Daddy, is Jesus' sandbox bigger than four sandboxes?" I nodded yes. "Is it bigger than 11 sandboxes? Is it bigger than eight-fifteen-seven sandboxes?"

"Silly boy," I said, playfully scrunching his hair.

Then Taylor giggled and asked to see *Winnie the Pooh.* I felt relieved. The probing questions of a three-year-old wrestling with the idea of God were worse than any seminary exam I had ever been asked to take. I found it easy to believe that a father's bad metaphor, tossed out in frustration or panic, could lead in later years to a heathen-pagan, crack-addicted, rock-n-roll drummer who calls his family only for bail. I had visions of Taylor on death row, being asked for any last words, and having him reply, "My father told me heaven was a giant sandbox—do I have to say more?"

For the next few weeks, Taylor was preoccupied with heaven and Jesus. He became, in fact, quite the little evangelist. After my wife told Taylor that only people who loved Jesus got into heaven, he became concerned about a neighbor friend he played with.

"Does Brad and his mommy love Jesus?" he asked her.

"I don't know, honey."

"Let's go tell them, Mommy. Tell them right now."

Later, on the porch swing, shortly after bopping his brother with his favorite stuffed animal, he crawled up in his grandmother's lap.

"Do you love Jesus, Grandma?" he asked, looking up at her.

"Yes, honey."

"Are you going to our heaven?"

"I'll go to the same heaven Taylor goes to," she replied.

"When we get there, we'll hold hands. Okay?"

Gradually, his attention shifted to Jesus. Questions, which usually came at bedtime, included: Does Jesus have a chainsaw? Does Jesus wear jammies? Does Jesus have a baseball hat? Do planes and birds go up to see Jesus in the sky? and, Is Jesus stronger than a Tyrannosaurus Rex?

Never once, of course, did Taylor question the actual existence of Jesus and heaven. He took it by simple faith, on the word of his parents, that both were real. What he was trying to do, however, was use his imagination to put flesh and bone on the concepts.

Young children, I believe, are, on the whole, full of belief. My own encounter with this came when I was six. My mother had given Tim and me each a Superman costume.

I do not recall right now why we received such gifts; maybe we were going to go trick-or-treating, or quite possibly my mother found them at a post-Halloween sale. In any case, I can remember that I wanted to wear mine everywhere—to Rink's Bargain City, to the library, to the Red Barn Hamburger Hut—to any number of places, it now occurs to me, where one might least expect to see Superman. Tim, on the other hand, was not as interested in his costume—I think he wore it once and threw it in the closet. This was fine with me; two Supermans was not only a bit repetitious, but in my mind's eye more than a little deflating and dishonest. Clearly, there was only one Superman.

I don't know why I liked this costume so much. Perhaps it was because I was a veritable runt of a boy, with eyelashes so long I couldn't wear sunglasses—the kind of child that, walking into a gift store, would get his cheeks pinched a minimum of a dozen times by women with handfuls of Hallmark cards. I wanted a tougher image.

More likely, however, I liked the costume because it gave me a sense of invincibility. With that costume on, cape tied around the neck with a granny knot, I was unstoppable. Gravity was just a word; villains were as good as dead; justice, if only I knew what it meant, was dished out like ice cream. (My parents began limiting my Superman appearances to places far removed from the general public after I tried to free an innocent hamster from imprisonment in the pet department at Hill's.)

Superman, the greatest power in the world, was most often limited to the area inside the railroad tie fence of my childhood home. Although I felt this a great injustice to the greater world at large, I learned to adjust. And then, unexpectedly, came my big chance. Probably because we were on vacation at a remote cottage near Lake Erie, my parents thought it safe to let me wear my Superman costume.

Sensing that this might be my last opportunity to prove my supernatural powers, I was on a keen lookout to do something heroic. Finally, my big chance came. It was late afternoon, and I was sitting on a boat dock that extended about eight feet into Lake Erie, watching my dad and my brother Jim fishing in a boat in the distance. Suddenly, there was a great amount of commotion—arms swinging, voices screaming, the rowboat visibly rocking. With my keen X-ray vision, I deduced Dad and Jim were in trouble, probably under a shark attack.

I did not hesitate. The fact I had not yet learned to swim was not of overwhelming importance. I do not recall either, with ten feet of a running start, whether I simply imagined myself flying to the rescue or, that, once in the water, I would swim naturally or whistle for Flipper. I probably did not think at all—I just *knew* Superman could do anything.

Fortunately for me, my sister, who I always regarded as sort of a red-headed Lex Luther, was swimming near the place where I chose to leap. As I was thrashing and sinking, she rescued me. As Superman lay gasping and wheezing on the dock, my father and brother, too far removed to know what had just occurred, excitedly pulled in a foot-long fish.

My mother, stripping my wet clothes off of me, said simply, "That's it, no more Superman." Still coughing up water, I could not find the energy to argue.

❦

Only children, of course, believe in Superman or wonder if Jesus is stronger than a Tyrannosaurus. Only they, lacking the facts to know better, would have such wild questions and impossible fantasies. Theirs is a faith, to be sure, but a faith twisted by a lack of concrete, linear logic. Clearly, we adults would say, not the same kind of faith we are supposed to have in a reasonable God.

Think again.

Consider, if you will, just some of the men and women listed in the Faith Hall of Fame of Hebrews 12.

- Abraham. By faith, he left family, community, and nation to set off for a "place"—a stranger living in a tent in the desert, with not even a hint of where he might end up. By faith, at the age of one hundred, with a barren, dried-up wife, he believed God was still able to deliver on his promise to make Abraham a father of many nations, and Isaac was born. By faith, he took this same improbable son, his only visible link to God's great promise, and was ready to kill him.

- Noah. By faith, he built a large boat on dry land, taking God at his word when he said it would rain, even though Noah did not have the slightest clue as to how much rain that might be.

- Moses. By faith, he turned down harems and jewels and knowledge for the opportunity to make friends with thankless slaves with dirt under their fingernails. By faith, he called down frogs, locusts, plagues, blood, flies, gnats, hail only to eventually find himself pinned between a raging sea and a raging army with only one fantastic way out.

- Daniel. By faith, with his life on the line, he interpreted the dream of a king. By faith, he told the most powerful person in the world that he was about to be squashed by a foreign nation. By faith, he refused to stop praying, only to find himself kneeling before the mouths of a few hungry lions.

The Bible goes on and on about faith. Jesus, when speaking of faith, said things that make a person cringe: He said that if a person with faith told a tree or mountain to move, it would do so. "I tell you the truth, anyone who has faith in me will do what I have been doing. He will do even greater things than these, because I am going to the Father" (John 14:12).

I have often found myself intimidated, puzzled, even infuriated over the strikingly unfamiliar landscape of faith as painted in the Bible. We find, in its contents, the audacity to pitch tents in the desert, or set foot on a seabed, or find joy in a cross, or bleed hope from a tomb, or throw a feast in the wilderness. The Bible teaches us that with faith, all things, in all circumstances, in any terrain, are possible.

Meanwhile, our almost twenty-first century world teaches us to set our expectations on flat and predictable scenery. We live in a world without imagination. Ours is a culture in which people speak in the current cliché, feed on the brains of experts, float weightlessly in a world of materialism, and live vicariously through athletes and actors and famous preachers. Our faith, the little we have, is in shopping or prescriptions or *Seven Steps to Something or Another*.

The world, of course, has always been a mess, but never have we tinkered so intricately before with the idea of futility. Busier than ever, we seem to be spinning our wheels for the sake of motion. Beyond belief, we are addicted and obsessed and neurotic. Without knowing it, we have broken down.

Science has become our Holy Grail. The facts tell us that we are no more than a collection of organs, cells, strands of DNA, enzymes, reactions, synapses. Dissected, without a soul, we feel the center slip. By mistaking the combination of the parts for the whole, science abandons the things that remain unseen: love, hope, trust, will, grace.

At the same time such a determinism drains us, it also resonates with the ring of truth. The world is clearly not right and, each one of us, no matter how hard we plan and scheme and try, is always breaking dreams against the cold wall of reality. Nothing, it seems, works as it is supposed to. A lump appears on a mother's nursing breast. A job collapses. A friend walks away. Tests are failed.

With the odds stacked against us by a gutless society and bloodless religion, is it not reasonable that we should retreat into the vapor of fantasy, or forge ahead in a steely, focused panic? Living, which is now out of the question, has been reduced to avoiding death—not just death, as in six feet under, but the little day-by-day deaths of trust and love and dreams that cause us so much pain.

Little deaths, final death. This is the soulless path of reason, the law of survival. Only grace, with its evocative and pungent aroma of life gives us the freedom to die. And even grace, by necessity and choice, came by way of a tomb. Eugene Peterson writes of the cross,

> Jesus Christ, God with us, enters this world of determinism and necessity, a world where nothing works out the way we want it or plan it or expect it and accepts the verdict: "My God, my God, why have you forsaken me?" But the submission [to crucifixion] is not cowardice; it is freely chosen strategy.

Jesus Christ, the son of God, absorbed evil and sin and wrath to himself and died a terrible death. Says poet W.H. Auden, "Christmas and Easter can be subjects for poetry, but Good Friday, like Auschwitz, cannot." Good Friday, that most ironic of oxymorons, is the unimaginably darkest day in all of time—past, present, and future. The horror in the cry, "My God, my God, why have you forsaken me?" is the hunger of each child who has ever starved, the pain in each bullet, disease, or cutting word, the accumulated violence of each war, rape, and molestation.

Yet, incredibly, Jesus' dying was also filled with faith, hope and love in that he trusted in God to raise him from the dead. In his life and death of faith, Christ broke the power of law and death. Romans 5:17 states: "For if, by the trespass of the one man [Adam], death reigned through that one man, how much more will those who receive God's abundant provision of grace and of the gift of righteousness reign in life through the one man, Jesus Christ."

The law, inflated with the spirit of abundant life, was fulfilled as grace. Where there once was only cold reason and lifeless law, as sure as the death of every man, there is now faith and grace, the possibilities as wild as what moves in an empty tomb.

Jesus' death and resurrection secured the promises of God. The power of sin and death disabled, those with faith are now also free to die. Secured in God's love, we are free to die to the self-seeking need for approval. Secured in God's protection, we are free to die to the constant churning of making our lives work. Secured in God's forgiveness, we are free to die to anger and bitterness that the world stirs in us. Secured in God's promise, we are free to die any kind of physical death. Secured in God's grace, we are free to live by faith. In the greatest equation known to humankind, law, reason, and science equal death. Grace equals resurrection.

At the church I attend, we have a children's sermon each Sunday. Each week, the worship team, of which I am a part, tries to come up with a creative way to communicate God to children. This is, without question, the most difficult part of the worship service for us to plan. We discuss, sometimes with deep conviction, such profound questions as, "Is it okay to wrap up a chewed-up dog toy and give it to one of the children as a present, and, if it is, will we be later responsible for the counseling bill?"

Usually it is hit-or-miss business. One particular Sunday, we came up with the less than brilliant and less than original idea of having someone talk to God and having God actually answer. The point we were trying to make was a worthy one, I think: God doesn't care *how* we talk to him, just that we *talk* to him.

During the children's sermon, things proceeded fairly smoothly until God spoke. (God, in this case, was a man by the name of Don who drives a red Saturn and is married to a woman named Donna.) Speaking through a wireless microphone in a room not visible to the children, the deep bass voice rang out.

Most of the children were wise to the trick (after opening up a present with a chewed-up dog toy in it, you would become a little skeptical, too), but three-and-a-half year old Logan was a notable exception. From the first reverberated word, Logan was convinced that this, indeed, was the very voice of God Almighty. Unfortunately, Don, getting maybe a little too much into divine character, decided to can the script and, with a great deal of authority, began to speak on nearly everything from Genesis to the End of Time. The longer he spoke, the more convinced Logan became of God's presence.

At first, Logan just sat, wide-eyed, slowly mouthing the words, "It's God." Then, braver, strengthened by the power of the Voice, he stood up, looking this way and then that, asking over and over, "God?" "God?" "God?" Eventually, he left the pack of children sitting on the platform and conducted his own personal search. "Where are you, God?" he began to ask. Intuitively, he walked toward the door that led to the room where God was speaking. He opened it, and with great respect, poked his head through. "I see God!" he said, running back through the door to tell his mommy.

God, meanwhile, was on a roll, unflappable, and completely unstoppable. In a way I am grateful for Don's oblivion for I fear that, if he had noticed, he might have said something like "Pay no attention to that man behind the curtain," and then the future of the church would have been permanently sealed. But what I will never forget is the look on little Logan's face. It was a look of a human who wanted, more than anything else in the world, to see God.

Each of us has experienced this same desperate longing to see God—to crawl up into his lap and rest, to have him softly sing a lullaby during times of pain, to hide in his shadow as he defies evil, to have him put our good works on display with refrigerator magnets.

But, for a little while, we have to live—or try to live—by faith. "Now faith," states Hebrews 11:1, "is being sure of what we hope for and certain of what we do not see." More specifically, according to John 6:29, "The work of God is this: to believe in the one he has sent."

This is no small task. Faith, in a world of tenacious and shiny things—missiles, promotions, tinsel, knives, coins—seems about as relevant and possible in our day-to-day lives as eating meat without teeth. What is the certainty of what we hope for, when we can only hope to make it to the end of the day? What can the evidence of things unseen possibly mean to us, when confusion spins us around so that we can barely figure out whose name is on the mailbox?

We are, none of us, much good at faith. Jesus, in one of his most frequent laments, says again and again with a weary and troubled heart, "Oh, you of little faith." It's just that the seen and practical are tangible, compared to the unseen and hope. They are something we can formulate an equation on or foundation around, or drive a boundary marker through, or fill with fuel and drive to the grocery store. In the battle between flesh and spirit—the war we never win—there is that certain draw to what can be held, manipulated, and controlled. Hope, in such a material world, is far too uncertain, and the unseen realities . . . well, far too unseen.

So, more often than not, we fall back into law and sin, the push and shove of everyday life, the insatiable demands of our own throbbing hearts.

Even though we have the great promises of God—food, shelter, abundant and eternal life—we often feel left in the lurch, waiting. We begin to assume that God needs some help. We may try to disguise it by speaking of responsibility or duty or obedience, but what we are doing, more than anything, is running after what is there for the taking. Exhausted, frustrated, we find it increasingly difficult to imagine that an unseen God can take care of our needs and desires.

We get reasonable and religious. The Pharisees, after all, had their facts straight. They wove law and doctrine, like ducks in a row, into a complex and striking set of rules, none of which in the slightest little bit depended upon anything unseen or hoped for. They lacked the imagination and humility to understand that God was already with them in Jesus Christ, freely offering grace, and they chose to continue stacking rule upon rule, vainly hoping that the pile would reach all the way to heaven, even though in the end, it was no larger and substantial than a dung heap. They could, at the very least, console themselves with the fact that it was *their* dung heap.

We all do it, cling to dung heaps. And in such a desperate and pathetic attempt to live, we die again. Sin, the ordering of the world on our own terms, always brings death. But here, again, is grace. After we have done the best we can do, or the worst we can do, and we lie crucified by our stupidity or fatigue or anger, we are still free to die. It is, then, perhaps, that we die well, for when we have exhausted our own puny resources and are further away than ever from what we desire, we are less likely to depend upon the effort of flesh. Cut loose from the idea that we can ultimately control anything, we are free once again to imagine what God can do. We are free to have faith.

Faith, by its very definition seldom appears practical. It requires stepping out onto the seemingly most fragile of limbs—living life based on unseen realities and the conviction of what is hoped for. Yet faith, the Bible clearly states, is at the center of all that matters. Without faith, nothing is possible; without faith it is impossible to please him.

But faith, like Rome, is not built in a day. Instead, it is built much in the same way that a child learns to build objects from an erector set—slowly, through trial and error. As I look back on my life of faith, I see a messy patchwork of failures and successes, the failures far outnumbering the successes.

We need to exercise our faith a little at a time. Most of the spiritual disappointments in my life have been a result of trying to do too much at once. This effort is as pathetic as the ninety-eight-pound weakling, who, after just one lesson from the Charles Atlas bodybuilding school, attempts to whip the evil bully with one quick swing. Things usually don't turn out too well, and the disappointment is always painfully remembered.

We need to be patient and bold, and, in a good sense, to experiment with our faith. Like my brother caught in the tree, we need to sense the desperation in our own efforts, and find the confidence to jump into the long and loving arms of God. The Bible, over and over, clearly tells us simple ways to move in faith and obedience. At first, it might be something like asking the Lord to help us make it through the day without swearing. Or, by faith, beginning to tithe, even though it requires some sacrifice. Or cutting back on the number of hours at work, even though we may risk losing a promotion. But we shouldn't try to change everything at once. We need to work to build spiritual muscle slowly, patiently, and with discipline.

Here is what happens. Say, in our faith experiment, we choose to begin tithing. As a discipline, we give ten percent of our money, and give it joyfully. Eventually, that faith will be rewarded, with blessings coming from unexpected directions: a closer relationship with family, a check from out of nowhere, a change in attitude about material possessions, a surer understanding of God as provider. As a test of faith in one area of our lives yields results, we learn that faith works, and that it is worth it. In our next experiment in faith, we will be working from a track record, as well as increased spiritual muscle. Slowly, in different aspects of our lives, we build our faith.

God is at work in different ways in each of our lives. In prayer and solitude, listen to the voice of God—in what area is he challenging you to faith? Once you have identified a specific area, say gossip, it is helpful to examine the Scriptures to see what God's standards are, as well as his specific promises of supernatural power. Then, in a real way, put your tongue on the line.

Most importantly, faith must be exercised in love. Our motivation to change must be because we love God, not because we want to impress him, secure his blessings, or make him love us more, all of which are impossible. Faith must be in the spirit of little Logan—a child desperately wanting to know the Father better, face-to-face.

In all such faith exercises, grace must be the environment. For it is grace that gives us the ability to be patient—Jesus Christ, not a ninety-eight-pound weakling, has the universe in his hands. And it is grace that gives us the freedom to fail, again and again, and in our failure, connect us to the life-giving realization that only God working through us will result in change. That is the paradox of faith.

I don't know, for sure, whatever happened to my Superman costume. We probably sold it at a garage sale, or tore it up to wash the car, or wrapped it in knots for our dog to pull on.

In my mind's eye, I remember the costume still—the color of blue, the buttons on the back, the length of the cape, the way the tied knot felt on my neck, the feeling of cotton, respect, power, energy.

I remember, too, the feeling of standing on that dock, examining the distance, fearing the chasm of water, and understanding that to get from here to there would take nothing less than a supernatural effort. When I heard what I thought to be the distress calls of my father and brother, I leaped.

It was a dunking of sorts. I am reminded of the verse: "We were therefore buried with him through baptism in order that, just as Christ was raised from the dead through the glory of the Father, we too may live a new life" (Romans 6:4).

I coughed up water, periodically, for the next few hours. My sister, who was hardly divine, had rescued me. My Superman costume, now dripping from a clothesline, had already been discarded in my mind as useless. I was thoroughly humiliated.

Yet was it any surprise, well into my adult life, that my imagination would lock on to Romans 13:14: "Clothe yourselves with the Lord Jesus Christ"?

9 CREATIVITY

Art does not reproduce the visible; rather, it makes visible.

PAUL KLEE ✺

Every third or fourth winter, usually on a day when the sun flashed like lightning on silver roofs, my father would surprise us with his art.

Up from a Saturday afternoon nap, wrapping himself in a couple of layers of winter clothes, he would disappear out the front door into a blinding, sun-washed blanket of white snow. If the temperature allowed it, Tim and I would dress quickly and follow him out into the winter's day; if not, we would watch from the dining room window. In the front yard, my father would work wordlessly—rolling, piling and packing snow. Meticulously, like a man toying with an idea just slightly out of reach, he shaped the snow this way, then that, looking for symmetry and angle. I remember the way the sun would catch in his searching eyes, the unsettled balance of light and intensity.

After shaping the snow into a vertical block, he would carefully pour on bucket after bucket of water. He would then wait, often going into the house for a cup of coffee or tea, only to return later with an ice pick, a chisel, and a file. Throughout the rest of the afternoon, he would sculpt patiently, consistently, stopping only to step back for a better and larger perspective.

My father would move from the bottom up, working first in broad strokes—rounding corners, cutting contours, shaving lines—ice-snow shards falling around him. Legs, abdomen, chest, arms, hands, neck, and head. The basic shapes completed, he would then concentrate on details. Here, his hands would slow considerably, almost as if someone had consciously thrown a switch, jamming his whole body into a lower, more focused, gear. If you happened to talk to my father during this period of his creation, he responded in a thick whisper, if he said anything at all. "Don't bother me right now," he seemed to be saying, no matter what words he may have actually uttered, as he formed muscles in the legs and arms, bones in the shoulders, ribs, and fingers.

When he came to the details of the face, my father usually stopped. About three feet away, eye to future eye, he would stand deep in thought, scanning each inch of his creation as if looking for the grain in the ice, or where, or if, a smile should fit.

From here, he usually traded his chisel for the small blade of his yellowed ivory pocketknife. Beginning with the eyes, he carefully carved—first eyes, eyelids, eyebrows, nose, forehead wrinkles, and then the curves and lines in the ears, mouth, lips, and sometimes teeth. For the most part, my father's ice creations were expressionless, like a child in sleep. He would often joke that he lacked the talent for creating such expressions, but I secretly think he understood the blankness of winter, and chose to transfer that blankness onto their faces.

His finished creations were quite diverse. Zelda was the first that I remember—a stout, rather muscular, but somehow tender young lady with a face tilted slightly to one side. Because of a freak heat wave, Zelda was with us for only a short while. The next was a monster of some sort, a cross between a man, an eagle, and a half-starved bear. Although perhaps the most artistic of my father's creations, I can't help but think this beast was more the result of an early and disastrous slip of the chisel than any sort of aesthetic considerations.

My favorite, however, was Frank. A veritable oaf of an ice man, Frank seemed, paradoxically, the most vulnerable of my father's creations. Kneeling in the snow, Frank was tilted back slightly, his body stiff, his gaze focused a bit too far above the line of the horizon. When you looked at him, there was an uneasy feeling that he did not know what to do with himself or with you, so he chose instead to stare off into an awkward and unoccupied space.

At the same time, Frank could surprise you. By a matter of coincidence or by careful planning of my father—I'll never know which—Frank was strategically placed so that the sun set directly behind him, giving him an unearthly and warm glow, the kind of purple-orange even the wildest and most undisciplined of artists would never dare imagine. At night, turning into the driveway after driving north on Old Dixie Highway, the headlights of our car would briefly catch Frank, turning him a blaze of unearthly white, like a veritable oaf of an angel.

It was from Frank that I first learned of light's power to transform.

Children are creative. Free from the pressure of survival and responsibility, not yet seduced by reason, alive in a world of wonder and possibility, a child gives birth to ideas in imagination, and has created. To them, a sculpted chunk of ice reflected off the headlights of a car is no longer what it appears, but a new creation.

Children are, in many ways, like artists. In their ignorance of what really is or what should be, or what will never be, they are fearless in their simplicity. Writes Aldous Huxley, "Only the most highly disciplined artist can recapture, on a higher level, the spontaneity of a child with its first paint-box. Nothing is more difficult than to be simple."

In simplicity, there is a freedom from clutter, a cleanness of line, a humility of perspective. One of the traits that Jesus found most praiseworthy was simplicity. In Matthew 11:25, he prays, "I praise you, Father, Lord of heaven and earth, because you have hidden these things from the wise and learned, and revealed them to little children."

The problem is, as they grow older, children lose their creativity. They are pressured to stay within the lines; they learn to calculate distance instead of exploring it; and, worst of all, they fall prey to fear.

Instead of accepting and appreciating what is unusual, which is the mainspring of creativity, they are taught to despise it.

When I was in fourth grade, Elizabeth sat one seat in front of me. Elizabeth, who took offense when you called her Liz or Beth, was an unusual girl. Desperately quiet, with skin as bland and flaky as a cracker, she seemed impenetrable behind straight, rusty-red hair, which was nearly always over her eyes. You had the feeling she was constantly covering up.

Elizabeth shook. I sat behind her in class and could see her hands visibly shaking, and when she was called upon to answer a question, her voice shook too, with that same half-timid, half-nervous kind of fragile excitement. She was the kind of girl who always seemed ready to break into tears, which in fact she often did.

Because we sat next to each other, and out of a mild sense of curiosity, I decided to try to get to know her. Secretly, so as to hide the fact from the rest of the class, I began meeting with Elizabeth under the first-floor stairwell on the walk back from recess. She was timid at first, her hair violently shaking as if it was on fire, but over time she began to open up to me.

Her father, I learned, had died when she was a baby, and her mother, as nearly as I could figure out, had been in the hospital a lot because she wasn't "quite right." Back then, I had no idea what an institution was and wouldn't have understood if someone had told me, but I knew by instinct that her mom was suffering. I could see it in her daughter's face.

Over the next month or two, Elizabeth and I continued our clandestine meetings under the stairwell. Eventually she learned to relax around me, calmed in trust, and soon considered me her friend, maybe her first ever. I began to like Elizabeth too. Underneath her pain and fear, she was caring and loyal and surprisingly creative. I remember I liked listening to the way she phrased her words.

Word got out. One afternoon, a classmate, stunned by getting hit in the head by a ball, stumbled into our mostly private meeting space. Even though he was dazed, it did not take him long to understand the magnitude of the scene that was in front of him. Robby with Elizabeth. "Ooooh," he said in a drawn-out whine, "Robby has Cooooties . . ." Up the stairs he ran, into the classroom, finally hushed only by a second warning from the teacher. "Robby has Cooooties . . . Robby has Cooooties . . . Robby has Cooooties."

Immediately, I was ostracized from the class, labeled as a loser. Although I felt the sting of falling from popularity, I still wanted to meet with Elizabeth—not so much out of pity, but because I had truly grown to appreciate her. As it turned out, our meetings under the stairwell were out of the question. The class, it seemed, had elected a person to spy out underneath the stairwell and report back on any hidden conversations between Elizabeth and me. In public, we stood even less of a chance. We were surrounded by chants of "First comes love, then comes marriage, then comes Cooooties in the baby carriage."

I was far from pure in my motivation. When the pressure of my friends increased, I slowly pulled away from Elizabeth. As our conversations became fewer and fewer, I could tell that Elizabeth was feeling the loss. Was it better to have no friends, or to have one and then lose him? She shook more than usual. Once, in a controlled kind of a panic, she asked to be excused from the class.

Then came the final break. As the teacher was presenting the class with new information of some sort, I noticed movement at my feet. Looking down, I saw a slow stream of water moving toward me. As I traced it back, I soon made the shocking discovery that it started from a pool of water directly under Elizabeth's seat. In her distress, she had lost control. She was peeing herself.

Without thinking, I jumped to my feet and let out a startled cry. It hadn't been my intention to draw attention to the situation, but it is my general belief that one tends to be less than rational when a stream of pee is headed one's way. It didn't take long for the class to catch on. In stunned silence, Elizabeth ran for the door, crying. For the next few minutes, as the teacher tried to calmly downplay the incident—"these things just sometimes happen"—no one said a word. It wasn't until recess, more than twenty minutes or so later, that the ridicule began. This time, feeling the pressure to separate myself from such an unthinkable act, I joined in.

I saw Elizabeth an hour or so later, walking with her aunt to the car. I watched them from a classroom window. Elizabeth had her head down and, only once, swiveling her head over her shoulder, did she look back. It was a quick glance, directed at no one in particular, but I can still see her face. Her eyes seemed to glow, not in anger, but sadness, like a pool of tears back-lit in a low sun.

I remember this story about Elizabeth because I am convinced that it was one of the most uncreative times in my life. I had the opportunity to create in Elizabeth a sense of respect and appreciation for her unique and God-given qualities. I had the chance to demonstrate an unconditional acceptance and empathy for the ways in which she had been unfairly damaged and judged. But, instead, I chose to be destructive, which is the antonym of creativity. I brought her more humiliation and judgment, all that much worse because I had called her a friend.

So often, for so many reasons, we fear to live creatively. Driven by our own personal needs for approval, love, security, and respect, we believe it is our responsibility to take care of ourselves. We live by public opinion or study the results of the latest survey or buy into the latest diet craze. We are bound within time and space and desire, no longer free to live creatively. The Elizabeths of the world, with seemingly so little to offer, are either dismissed or run over in the push and shove of need.

Faith, stirred by the imagination, is the one thing that allows us to live creatively. At its core, faith begins in divine promise. God told Abraham that he would make him a father of many nations. He told Moses that he would take him to the promised land. He told Joshua that the walls would fall. And he says to each one of us, "I will take care of you."

God's promises free us. No longer is it necessary to accumulate possessions to validate our worth. No longer is it necessary to influence the right friends so that we can realize our own importance or to slave and toil and sell your soul for a sense of security. No longer is it necessary to devastate the Elizabeths of the world.

Living creatively doesn't necessarily refer to the way we paint on canvas or build sand castles at the beach, but to how we relate to each other in a deeper way, in the brush strokes of one soul on another. Jesus said that the entirety of the law hangs on two commandments: Love God, love others. Love, if it is anything at all, is moving beyond the narrowness of self into the expansive and terrifyingly free world of creativity. We are faced with choices, opportunities, potential, free to build into our own lives, and the lives of others, the love of God.

When I was nine, I made my dad a Creeple People for his fortieth birthday. For those of you uninitiated in the world of baked plastic, this may take some background.

Tim and I began, of course, with Creepy Crawlers. Sometime in the 1960s, unrestricted by any laws requiring their products to be safe, a large toy manufacturer came up with the idea of allowing children to bake plastic.

The essence of the process was pouring what Tim and I called plastic goop into metal molds. Plastic goop, a liquid the consistency of pancake syrup, at first came in four basic colors and, then, in an ever-growing desire to give children options and at the same time increase profits, the manufacturer began to offer what seemed like an infinite numbers of colors. After pouring the plastic goop into the molds, which were held by a handle similar to what you would find on a french fry bucket, they were then lowered onto a square oven similar to, and no less dangerous than, a hot plate. As it cooked, the plastic goop would change in hue, darkening from the outside in. Once the color was consistent, the Creepy Crawler was done.

There were several different kinds of molds, each with anywhere from two to five Creepy Crawlers—spiders, lizards, beetles, frogs, centipedes. My personal favorite was the bat, with its careful symmetry of wing and evil eyes; Tim, if I remember right, had quite a fondness for the frog, which, at no extra charge to the consumer, came with some pretty cool warts.

Tim and I loved Creepy Crawlers. We created an entire upstairs hallway kingdom with them. At first, gentle and caring, they lived together on one island blanket. Then, led by an embittered octopus who had lost a couple of its legs to Tuffer, an insurrection occurred. The octopuses, frogs, spiders, and June bugs split from the main kingdom and went to live on their own island. Pretty soon, as the sad story always goes, the islands were at war with one another, hurling insults, then blocks and Lincoln logs. Any Creepy Crawlers turned upside down on impact were considered dead.

We warred, unless bedtime interrupted us, until the last Creepy Crawler was left on its belly.

Fortunately we were rescued from our violence by our greed. About a year or so after introducing Creepy Crawlers, the company that made them, buoyed by a desire for producing more creative outlets for children, introduced Creeple People. Although the basic idea remained the same—pouring colors of plastic goop into molds—the concept had advanced to the next level. Instead of creating separate creatures, Creeple People offered the opportunity to bake body parts and, like Dr. Frankenstein, to assemble the parts together into various races. Somewhat to our disappointment, the body parts stuck to the basics of legs, arms, and head, but, still, the overall idea of piecing together life was overwhelming to us.

We simply *had* to have the Creeple People set. But— in surely what was a production slip-up on the part of the manufacturer—Creeple People required an entire new set of ovens, molds, and even plastic goop. Dad and Mom, resorting to the obvious, reminded us that money didn't grow on trees. If we wanted the set, we would have to buy it ourselves. Great. I had about fifty-seven cents to my name, most of which I had gotten by searching in sofa cushions or by returning pop bottles. And Tim, like a washed-out addict, had spent all of his money on bottles of plastic goop to increase his Creepy Crawler troops.

Our backs to the wall, we got creative. In order to raise the funds to buy the Creeple People set, we began to sell black market Creepy Crawlers on the school play-ground. At first, we stuck to the basics—solid-colored creatures with no extras. Three cents for the small creatures, a nickel for the big creatures, and a dime for the horny toad, which was quite enormous.

Even Tim and I could not have imagined the demand for our products. Spurred by a waiting list, we branched into a new, customized product line. Tell us what you wanted in a creature, and we could supply it. A black beetle with red legs, no problem. A rainbow bat with a safety pin baked in its back so that you could wear it on a sweater, a cinch. A green horny toad with red warts, you got it.

Eventually, our business grew so large that Tim and I had to take on specialized roles. Tim was the president and creator; I was the salesman. For my role, I received a generous twenty-five percent split (and a black eye courtesy of one of our customers, who was sold a defective centipede missing several legs).

Unfortunately, our business was shut down after one of Tim's fifth-grade classmates bought a Creepy Crawlers set of his own and entered into competition. The elementary school principal, unable to handle price gouging by ten-year-olds, stepped in and shut down both businesses. "Kickball is fun," I remember him telling me.

By then, however, Tim and I had more than enough money to buy the Creeple People hardware. I still remember the thrill of bringing it home from the store, and, under a low light in our closet, baking our first Creeple Person.

The idea was rather simple. The baked arms and legs were U-shaped with hands and feet extended at the ends. These both had a hole in the middle, which you could stick a pencil through (available at extra cost). Over the eraser head went the Creeple People head, which was large and goofy looking.

The head, we soon discovered, was the creative challenge. Baked in hinged halves, with a hole at the top to insert the optional Creeple hair (available at extra cost), the front and back of the head were brought together at the small, O-shaped neck, which was connected by a Creeple People ring (available at extra cost). There were several different head molds (available at extra cost), and the potential for creativity was virtually unlimited.

About two months after our purchase came my father's birthday. Since I had spent all my money on Creeple People accessories, I could not afford to buy him a gift, so, after much deliberation I decided to make him a Creeple Person. I spent an inordinate amount of time in my bedroom closet the night before his birthday creating just the right combination. Around me were strewn the sad corpses of slightly flawed Creeple People parts—a too red set of arms, an overcooked head, a webbed foot. Dad, after all, deserved the best. I wanted this Creeple People to be as nearly perfect as possible.

Finally, late into the night, I finished my creation. He was, to my overly tired eyes, the epitome of the Creeple People race: orange hair fashioned into a perfect beehive, a mostly green head with an accent of purple swirl, arms and legs molded around paper clips for variable positions, fingernails and toenails outfitted in sublime splashes of red. I slept deeply that night, dreaming of my father's surprised and adoring face.

❧

True artists do not create, in the fully technical sense of the word. Rather, through arrangement or contrast or use of light, they take what has already been created and help us to see it from a new perspective. Acts of creativity, then, are a response to a particular environment.

If we wish to live creatively—giving artfully through our gifts and our selves—we must first examine our spiritual environment. Why? Because creativity blossoms in an environment of grace—the unexpected and mind-boggling news that God keeps his promises, no matter what we do. In the overwhelming hues and tones and colors and textures of such an environment, we are free to create—to use our lives, *all* of our lives, to live in loving response to God.

Keep a diary during the next week. After each day, record what you did during the day—just a few notes on events, moments, frustrations, activities, etc. After the week is over, go back and evaluate the information in your diary. Ask yourself, at the very least, the following questions: How much of what you did reflected the creative life of fulfilling the two great commandments? How much of what you did was focused—directly or indirectly—on meeting personal needs?

To answer these questions, we must deal with the often subtle and deeper issues of motivation. In my own life, for example, I find that I am a master of disguising the promises of God behind my own will. If I don't do *this*, God will not provide. If I fail to recognize *that*, I will invalidate a promise of God. And, in the end, I subtly but finally come to the startling conclusion that God cannot be trusted at all. I find myself trapped, once again, in the law.

I am not advocating we should all leave our jobs, dump the housework, quit the evangelism committee, and move to Cancun. But, as I move deeper into my own adult life and feel less and less creative, it has been useful to look at my motivations. Do I live the way I do because I want to honor, worship, and glorify God, or is it because I fail to trust God for the basic promises of life and feel the need to secure them myself? More often than not, I *need* my life for selfish reasons—to pump up a sagging ego, to build a savings account, or to make people love and respect me.

When we depend upon things outside the promises of God for our fulfillment, our lives get cluttered, not only with impure motives, but with the external validations of self—the collection of possessions, awards, titles, things yet to be accomplished. In seeking to develop a creative environment, we must attempt to simplify our lives. We must seek to look at the world again as freshly as a child with his first set of paints.

Part of how we can do this is through simply removing things from our lives. Ask yourself these tough questions:

- Do I really need a home with a pool that, although providing us with a certain amount of

respect and comfort, robs us of time and perspective?
- Do I really need the job promotion that has been stealing me away from my wife and children?
- Do I really need to involve myself in another ministry if my life is already out of balance from doing too many good things?

By eliminating clutter from our lives, we will discover the slavery of the motivation that drove the clutter in the first place. In his song, "Things We Leave Behind," Michael Card writes,

With Jesus, our only possession
Then giving becomes our delight
And we can't imagine the freedom we find
From the things we leave behind

Simplicity provides a cleanness of line. Creativity happens when we are stripped to the basics. Like my father on a cold winter morning, with hammer, chisel, chunk of ice, and his certain knowledge of potential, so should we as Christians be chipping and shaping and loving others more closely into the image of God. Only in simplicity of life and perspective are we free to do so. This is the art of life.

A few years ago I went exploring in the attic of my parents' house. I found some of my old second-grade math papers—my mother only kept the A or A+'s—as

yellow and fragile as the wings of dead butterflies. There was my old Stingray bicycle, with sponge erupting from the seat, and that same obnoxious bell that used to drive my mom to near hysteria.

And, deep in the corner tucked behind a fan, there was a shoe box wrapped in rubber bands. Opening it, I immediately recognized some of the artifacts of my father's work on the railroad: a couple of old work orders, a time sheet, an old pay stub.

As I ruffled through the papers, something at the bottom of the box caught my eye. Reaching down, I touched something rubbery and strange. When I pulled it out, there it was: the world's best Creeple People—orange-haired, a body of green accented with purple swirls, paper clips sticking rudely out of arms and legs. I was stunned. *How ridiculous looking,* was my first thought.

But as I reflected, I saw things differently. I pictured my father, deep into his work, stopping to look at this gift. Far from a work of art, it served as a visible reminder of his son's love.

10 *LOVE*

Love does not consist in gazing at each other but in looking outward together in the same direction.

ANTOINE DE SAINT-EXUPERY ❦

I would have never suspected it from my parents, especially not at Paul's, in between the shelves with the potato chips and the charcoal lighter.

Paul's was what we called the little grocery, which, if not in the middle of nowhere, was next to it, in the "town" of Mortimer, which consisted of four houses, a railroad station, and a restaurant/bar that changed its name every six months—the North Wind, the Black Stallion, the Panther.

Paul himself, possibly to balance such a drift of names, never bothered to call his store anything. What with the gas pumps out front, the Pepsi sign over the door, and the advertisements in the window, Paul was probably under the impression that the building cast enough hints as to its purpose and, if people were really in need of a sign, they would have probably headed for the Findlay A&P anyway. Timid and bespectacled and prudent, Paul never impressed me as a man given to any unnecessary flashing.

The store, too, was flat, tiny, disheveled, unvarnished. Paul was not particularly gifted at organization—the pickles could just as easily have been found next to the fishhooks as the ketchup. Even though we were as familiar as anyone with Paul's, I don't believe there was ever a time when any member of our family didn't have to ask for the location of at least one item. "Ahh, Paul, where are the onions today?" He would point, looking up with as much of a hint of disgust as a timid man could muster and mutter, "Second aisle, third shelf, next to the paper cups." Of course.

We liked both Paul and Paul's. In the man and the store, we sensed a loose, eclectic, almost stubborn pushing back of something—time, reality, a loose brick or two? Yet, in what remained, in the haphazard and random order, there was the reeking of character. In addition to a running bill, we had a certain amount of respect for this man, this place.

That's why my parents took me by surprise. Tim and I, as was our custom when Dad and Mom said we could, had each been picking out a bottle of water-cooled pop from Paul's double-hinged pop machine. Normally, this took up to fifteen minutes or so; neither Tim nor I wanted to squander such a taste extravaganza on an incorrect choice. But this being an uncommonly hot day, I sacrificed the ecstasy of choice for a quick purging of my thirst. In looking back, I suspect that my parents believed that they had plenty of time.

In any case, as I turned a corner on the wood floor, there they were. My father was leaning against the potato chips, holding my mother tightly in his arms; they were kissing passionately. I noticed the sweat on their foreheads.

My first reaction was instinctual; I looked for Paul. I was convinced that, had he known exactly what was taking place between aisles two and three, he may have committed any number of unreasonable acts—muttered under his breath, dropped dead from a heart attack, or even, in a moment of uncontrolled passion, thrown a beef jerky at them. Fortunately, Paul was ringing up another customer.

In all of my ten years of existence, I had never seen my parents acting so . . . well . . . intimate. When it came to showing a great deal of public affection, they were always conservative—a peck, a quick hug, a held hand. I always knew that my dad and mom loved each other deeply, but I never suspected, or even thought about, *this* kind of love. And right in the middle of Paul's, of all places. It gave me the heebie-jeebies.

When my parents seemed undistracted by my appearance, I quickly ran away, deciding the best course of action was to retreat to the back seat of our car, a yellow-green, plump Buick.

A few minutes later, my family emerged, led by Dad and Mom, who were laughing as if it were a full moon, unruffled except slightly in their clothes.

"Did you have a good pop?" my dad turned and said to me in the back seat. With some hesitation, I nodded yes. He winked, and I knew, in that one moment of an otherwise common day, the fierce and tender intensity of the love between my mother and father.

Elizabeth Barrett Browning once wrote, "Whoso loves, believes the impossible." The words have a ring of truth, not because love seems so high and mighty, but because it seems, in the spinning of the world, so tenuous and frail.

Seldom does love, stripped of raw emotion, lift us to the transcendent mountain tops; rather, it dwells on the common and often dreadful plains of day-to-day life. Seldom does it cleanse the heart of fear; rather, it moves like a whisper in the long valley between desperation and longing.

The shock of finding my father's and mother's passion was not in the passion itself, but in the contrast of the surroundings. Between the potato chips and the charcoal lighter, in a tiny, wooden-floored store without a name, on a hot August day, under the nose of a tiny, half-scrabbled man, with children at the pop machine, there was this dangerous and fragile throwing of red spark, like the threat of fire, the melting of two souls into one. At Paul's, of all places.

In a world septic and spiked with careless moments, who can imagine such a flawed tenderness, such a ripe ripping against the grain? In a culture strung out and bored, what is this kind of eruption that is kindled with years? In a heart seized with need, anger, longing, the pumping of self, where do such delicate seeds of love take root?

Love is outrageous, impossible, in its tenderness in a tough world. Listen to 1 Corinthians 13: "Love is patient, love is kind. It does not envy, it does not boast, it is not proud. It is not rude, it is not self-seeking, it is not easily angered, it keeps no records of wrongs. Love does not delight in evil but rejoices with the truth. It always protects, always trusts, always hopes, always perseveres." Can you imagine the possibility of such love?

❧

When I was born, a doctor told my parents that I would be prone to upper respiratory tract infections. If they weren't careful with me, I might develop serious complications. I am not certain how this man knew this, and I wish, even if it would have been possible to arrive at such a factual conclusion, he would have kept it to himself.

Because of this man's prophecy, one of things I most associate with my childhood is the smell of Vicks VapoRub. It is my humble estimation that for at least one third of the nights my mother put me to sleep, I was wearing a rag, pinned behind my neck, soaked in Vicks. If I so much as sniffled or sneezed during the day, I would be submitted to the same treatment.

On the whole, I must confess, this is not an altogether unpleasant memory. My father, who I have always suspected of being a frustrated pharmacist, would retrieve the half-gallon size blue-green jar and place it in a pan of water on the stove to warm.

My mother would then take the warmed Vicks and rub it into my chest and neck area. The smell, the gentle massage of my mother's hands, and the warm penetration of the Vicks combined for a pleasant and relaxing bedtime ritual. All the while, my mother would tell me how much she loved me.

There were, of course, more than a few drawbacks to the Vicks strategy. In much the same way that a hangover reduces the pleasure of drunkenness, the mornings after Vicks were singularly miserable. First, there was the feel. The warmth long since dissipated, and the Vicks rubbed deep into each pore by a night of turning over in bed, there remained a clammy, sticky, cold moisture, much as if a dog had entered my bedroom during the night and licked my chest.

Then, too, there was the sick couch. Tucked away in the den, right next to my sister's hi-fi, was an old, green sofa with a perpetually musty smell. This was where anyone would lay when we were sick or, as often was my case, when I was suspected of being sick. I am not sure how the tradition of the sick couch began, but I suspect it was because the den was located between the kitchen and dining room, thus making it convenient for my mother to check on a sick child in between passes.

After a night of Vicks, my mother would put me on the sick couch, listening, I was sure, for any sneezes, coughs or sniffles. If I could go for thirty minutes or so without doing any of the aforementioned, I was free to get down and play. The sick couch was my temporary prison.

There *were* times, when I was more seriously ill, that the sick couch became a haven of sorts. I was nine when I came down with the measles. During the next three days, the sick couch was my home. For such extended stays, my mother would bring her special touches to the faded, threadbare couch by wrapping the pillows in a multicolored striped blanket. She would drape a light blue blanket over me and, more times than not, lift the ban from our dog getting up on the couch. Tuffer would sleep next to me, his head usually lying on my stomach.

For two to three days during my bout with the measles, I ran a high fever and felt generally miserable. In between long periods of sleep, I would emerge into a foggy consciousness, see the room spinning around me, and call out for my mother. She would come over, cooling my face with a wet towel, and tell me that I would be fine. Reassured, I would fall back into my alternately wild, then blank dreams.

But what I remember most was her kiss. Only half-awake, wrestling with the bent shapes of fever, I could feel my mother's presence, even if I was not consciously aware of it. First, her smell, then a whisper, and finally her lips, as delicate as rose petals, lingering on my forehead. With such a kiss, my mother melted into my dreams the way pink moves into purple. In such a harsh sickness, she showed such tender love.

In the Gospels, the love of Christ is never protected. It is there—in all of its tenderness, in all of its crystal-like frailty—in a world that crushes love under the gravity of sin like a flower under a falling boulder. I cringe, sometimes, at Christ's openness in the Bible, his lack of argument, his foolish, wild love.

We see him at the tomb of Lazarus, brokenhearted over death, raising his friend back to life. We observe, in the middle of such love, the mumblings, the strategies against him.

We watch him heal the ten lepers, freeing them from a prison of disfigurement, shame and exile. We see them forget Jesus and we shiver over the depths of such cold hearts, feeling the blood running cold in ours. Ask for your due, we growl, but Jesus revels in the love of one.

We watch him press toward Jerusalem, toward the hard-hearted accusations, toward the blood-hungry hill, toward the cross. We see him before Pilate, a ruler who only *thinks* he is powerful, and we want to put words in Jesus' mouth—to have him say "They are liars, these accusers." We want him to defend himself, to set things straight. But he is mostly silent, allowing love to speak for itself.

We see him at the cross. Golgotha. At his death we find the mobs of people who once called him friend. "Father, forgive them," he yells in anguish, "they do not know what they do." Love incarnate, betrayed and forsaken, on its last breath, chooses to be broken. He could have yelled for angels but instead he offered up love, like a candle in a dark, pouring rain.

Ours is a world in which love always seems overwhelmed—even the Son of God was battered under the weight of wickedness. The head that thought of only love wore a crown of thorns. The back that bore our sins was whipped. The hands that healed and touched, the feet that walked the dusty roads looking only for faith, the heart that broke in sorrow—all of these were pierced, run through with iron. In a broken and brutal world, love, in its most pure and potent form, is crucified.

Where does that leave those of us who wish to kiss, who try to love?

LOVE

I don't remember, for sure, what my father had accused me of doing. I only recall sitting on my bed feeling the red sting in my butt, and more so, the ache in my heart. I had been punished for something that I did not do.

My father, as was his custom when he disciplined, first gave me the opportunity to confess and ask for-giveness for what I had done. As hard as I pleaded, I could not convince him that, this time at least, I was not guilty. He then explained to me that he would have to spank me, and listed the reasons why. I remember breaking into a whine, then a scream, and then a kick-ing, righteously indignant tantrum. Far from convinc-ing my father of my innocence, these acts only served to increase the intensity of my punishment.

As he was leaving the room, I turned to him, the tears silently flowing down my cheeks, and said, "But, Daddy, I really didn't do it." He patted my head and told me to think about what I had done. When I was ready to tell the truth and say I was sorry, he said, I could come down and join the family.

Fat chance. I was innocent and deeply hurt. I sat in my bed by the window for hours, watching the light bleed from the sky and a slow rain move in from the west. I moved from a sadness that my father didn't believe what I said, to an anger that desired revenge. "I hate him," I muttered under my breath, for this was the only way I knew to get back at him.

But more than wanting the wrong redressed, I wanted my father to hear me, to trust me, to believe me. The hurt in my butt had faded; the pain in my heart had grown. For hours on end, I sat there, watching the slow rain, moving between tears and anger. In my own childish way, I wanted justice.

I cried myself to sleep.

In my troubled sleep, I felt a hand on my shoulder. "Robby," the voice said in a whisper, "Robby, wake up." It was my father. There were tears in his eyes.

My father explained to me that he had discovered that I was innocent. "I am so sorry, Robby," he said. "Please, forgive me." I don't recall too many times in my childhood that my father cried, but this was one of them. He took me in his arms and hugged me. I patted him gently on the shoulders and said that it was okay, that I still loved him.

For the longest time, we were silent in each other's arms. I remember the way the rain sounded on the window, and my father's troubled breathing. Finally, slowly, he pulled himself away and looked me in the face. "Do you forgive me, Robby? I am so sorry I hurt you like this. I love you." I told him that I forgave him.

He kissed me on the forehead with a depth of passion that still echoes in my heart today, and we walked off, hand-in-hand, father and son, to rejoin the family.

Against all odds, against all hope, against the wildest of dreams, love crucified, arose. Resurrection is the unlikely and unimaginable beginning after the final end. Where once love was delicate, crushed in the terror of the world, resurrection reveals it to be tenacious, unsinkable, and eternal, woven in the heavens.

Falsely accused, the Son died, paying the penalty for the sins of others. Isaiah 53 boldly states, "It was the Lord's will to crush him and cause him to suffer." The Father freely sacrificed his Son to an undeserved punishment. The Son joyfully accepted the undeserved punishment of the Father. Only that kind of love stirs the power of resurrection.

Can you imagine the embrace of Father and Son, the tears of joy at the repentance of one sinner uttering the words "Please forgive me"? Can you imagine Father and Son, hand-in-hand, bringing together the family of God? Can any of us ever imagine the sheer power of love?

To have faith is to believe in the possibility of such an impossible love. Out of being divinely loved ourselves, we are to desire to follow the path of love: death, then resurrection. At the core of love is Philippians 2:3: "Do nothing out of selfish ambition or vain conceit, but in humility consider others better than yourselves." Love, if it is to be genuine, must die to selfish needs and desires.

In a mad and broken world, such genuine love is like pitching a small tent at the base of an avalanche— in dying to self, we are, more times than not, simply crushed. In an office full of ladder climbers, imagine the love of a father who stoops to play with his children. In a family void of heart connections, imagine the child who takes in an elderly mother with Alzheimer's. In a culture full of money and material possessions, imagine the woman who moves to a third world country to care for sick children. In a world full of missiles, imagine the man with the courage to seek peace with another.

Love, in the massiveness and confusion of sin and evil, seems such a small act in the midst of our day-to-day living. Death to self is always painful, and, in the end, if love blooms at all, is so small. It is easy to just give up, to fulfill our own selfish impulses, to call it a day. Or a year. Or a life.

But we must never forget the power of resurrection that comes through those small acts of love. What we do reflects who we are. In Galatians 6:8–9, Paul encourages Christians to continue to love despite the seeming futility of it: "The one who sows to please his sinful nature, from that nature, will reap destruction; the one who sows to please the Spirit, from the Spirit will reap eternal life. Let us not become weary in doing good, for at the proper time we will reap a harvest if we do not give up."

Acts of love, then, are like the life that comes from seeds. What is required, first, is death. Jesus says in John 12:24, "I tell you the truth, unless a kernel of wheat falls to the ground and dies, it remains only a single seed. But if it dies, it produces many seeds." In death, in just one tiny seed, lies the latent power of resurrection.

My youngest son, Ethan, is two and a half. He is, by nearly anyone's account, a walking paradox of a child. One second he can be spearing his older brother with a piece of a Hotwheels race track; the next, he is hugging his mother as if his life depended upon it.

I watch him with wonder, and maybe a little bit of fear. What is love to a small child? Is it not simply a way of getting needs met? Yet there he is, in his Pooh Bear jammies, lips extended in the shape of a small tulip, wanting to give kisses. I see the way his eyes move, searching for the light in the eyes of others, then connecting and kissing. "Hug," he will then mostly likely say, throwing his arms gently around you.

I do not understand how such kisses can be so freely given—how, after he has been disciplined for hurting his brother, he can kiss just as tenderly as before. It is amazing to me that even in the fire of such deep and contradictory action, he can abandon himself in what seems a genuine love.

Yet, in each adult, is there not that same struggle? Are we not, in a slightly less extreme fashion, just like my little Ethan—slicing a brother with a cutting word, and then, arms and lips extended, wanting so desperately to kiss purely? Do we not, each one of us, move back and forth between tantrum and desire, anger and longing? Isn't there, in any given day, that battle between taking and giving, between desiring to do things on our own terms and getting lost in the love of another? And how are we, given such internal conflict, supposed to develop a consistent attitude and practice of love?

First, in order to love, we must understand what it is like to *be* loved. If someone does not understand what it means to be loved unconditionally, then asking them to love is like asking a man without a mouth to talk. It is impossible.

We learn love by being touched by it. In my own childhood and now in the life of my own children, I have learned that love is more a response than an action. What of those kisses in my childhood—my parents at Paul's; my mother's tenderness in the fog of my fever; my father's tear-filled confession? These kisses were small things, nearly invisible, practically unconscious, but in them were such higher realities: In the world of mundane and sweltering August days, passion; in the grip of sickness, a healing touch; in the agony of loss, forgiveness. As I matured, my love became a response, a testing of what my parents had already shown to be reality.

Second, if we seek to continually learn about love, we must never stop being children. Wide-eyed, full of trust, we should be open to invisible possibilities. The Apostle John, perhaps better than any other, understood the relation of little children to love. I love the imagery John uses of little children, both in their relation to the beloved disciple as well as to the Father. In 1 John 3:1, he writes, "How great is the love the Father has lavished on us, that we should be called the children of God!"

Third, it is critical to remember that, ultimately, love has its starting point in the love of the Father. How great is the love the Father has lavished on us! The word *lavish,* at its root, means to wash or to shower. God bestows his love on his children like a rain in May, in extravagant and grace-filled abundance.

When we experience the love of the Father, we, with the hearts of children, will be free and empowered to love. When we understand the cross, will we not naturally respond with a passionate love for our loved ones? When we watch God give of himself until he has nothing left to give, will we not be willing to suffer also, in the name of love? When we understand that love is at the center of all of creation, will we not move in from the sidelines?

Only as we are rooted and abandoned in the love of God, will we be able to love, for it will be God himself who loves. By welcoming him—even though you still experience all the limitations of sin—you yourself will experience life on God's terms. It stands to reason, doesn't it, that if the alive-and-present God who raised Jesus from the dead moves into your life, he'll do the same thing in you that he did in Jesus, bringing you alive to himself?

Finally, we must develop a realistic attitude about love—one that is neither too grand or too pessimistic. If we begin with the idea that love is always a grand and remarkable gesture—like falling on a grenade or having a banner pulled at five thousand feet by an airplane—we will quickly become discouraged, for love is seldom so grandiose. Rather, love most often exists in tiny, day-to-day, familiar acts. The seeds love throws can be as small as a word of encouragement on the phone, a confrontation of a friend who is in sin, or a shoulder to hold on to. Buried, tiny, and seemingly insignificant, such seeds of love have the power to live forever.

In third grade, I fell in love with Sherri Baker. She was red-haired, red-freckled, and only slightly taller than me, the smallest boy in my class. At first, I didn't know what was happening to me—I thought I was coming down with some exotic childhood disease. My heart fluttered a good deal.

This was in Mrs. Buechner's class; Sherri sat next to the window, the light tumbling down her hair. I think, but I am not sure, that Sherri started to like me in first grade, way back when Mrs. Pusey had the class create a life-size cardboard cutout of one of the students, which happened to be me. Even though I was chosen, in no small part, because I was the runt of the class and Mrs. Pusey could cut her cardboard expenses, I think Sherri developed a fondness for me—or, at least, the cutout image of me.

At a time when such love was dangerous, thought to be the cause of Cooties or blindness or stunted growth, Sherri and I became an item. When the class lined up in pairs to walk to the lunchroom or the playground, Sherri and I were there, hand-in-hand. During recess, we played together, even though for the life of me I can't imagine what kind of games we played. I even gave Sherri a custom-designed Creepy Crawler ring—an orange-and-black bat (our school colors) with a bread wrapper wire baked in its back.

For such a love, we endured it all: kickballs thrown at us at recess; oogley eyes of classmates at cafeteria lunches; overly cute smiles of adults that hinted such a love would never last.

We took advantage of every opportunity to express our fondness. We passed silly notes, folded into silly designs, through our friends. We gave each other towering Valentines, the biggest in the pack of sixty-four. And, whenever we could be, we were together.

I remember one evening especially. The Van Buren Black Knights football team was playing their conference rival, the Cory-Rawson Hornets. Sherri's brother, Terry, was one of the stars of the team.

Sherri and I, as we had planned during the day, met at the far goal line—each of us, for the sake of cover, walking with a friend. We held hands. It was one of those raw, early November evenings, the leaves blowing through the parking lot and playground, imagined voices of the winter to come. At halftime, we shared a hot dog and a hot chocolate.

Even though the game was exciting, I do not know, for the life of me, who won. Sherri and I left the game walking one unmittened hand in one unmittened hand through the school yard, resting in each other's company.

We did not do much or say much. In the distance we could hear the pulsing of cheers, the soft globe of light, the dry, floating voice of a man in the crow's nest: "Huffman the ball carrier, tackled by Roberts." Under a wild moon and the silver racing of clouds, Sherri and I kissed our first kiss. By the sparks that danced in my spine, I knew then, for the first time, the true power in love.

Traveling Home

Home interprets heaven. Home is heaven for beginners.

CHARLES PARKHURST 🪬

Doug was, for one spring and one summer, my best friend.

He came into my life from out of nowhere—Houston, I think he said once—and settled with his family into a gray, arthritic house in Mortimer, across from Paul's grocery.

I liked Doug from the start and knew he would become my best friend, even though I'm not sure how I knew that. He came near the end of the school year, wearing his crewcut as his only defense, half-ambling, half-stumbling into our fourth-grade class.

Coming to a new school in April didn't leave Doug a great deal of opportunity to make friends before summer break. Most of my classmates seemed wary of him, like they might act around anything unfamiliar or unexpected—a carrot in a cereal box, for instance. A nervous and unsettled energy surrounded their half-conscious avoidance of him.

Doug had a slight accent, but not nearly as much as Lyndon Baines Johnson, and Texas, which I would have thought to be a large and distinctive part of him, seemed only a hitch in the corner of his smile. He could, however, swagger in the most surprising ways.

We became fast friends. I remember riding my bike down to Paul's in the April rains that spring. At first he seemed reluctant to show me inside his house, electing instead to head across the street to get a jawbreaker or, when we had the money, a water-cooled Coke. Sometimes, we would head down the railroad tracks, the smell of erupting green and rain-soaked creosote exploding around us.

Doug preferred coming to my house. What tied us together, so quickly and deeply, was our imaginations. In my backyard world of lime-striped baseball field, electrified tree house, pony rides, sandbox towns, and basement spaceships, Doug played with a sense of tenacity. While imagination was natural for me, for him imagination seemed necessary, like breathing. I had never met anyone before like Doug, who seemed to draw breath off play.

By the summer, we were constant companions. Our play, while always at the center of what we did, expanded into deeper areas of our lives. As much as Doug enjoyed a water volcano in the sandbox, he came to appreciate sitting in front of a fire in our living room, quietly watching my family interact. He never said much and, when he did, he often stuttered. My dad and mom, I remember, wondered how a boy could be so quiet and so aggressive at the same time.

Eventually, Doug let me into his home. At first, it was when his parents weren't around. His father, who made his living as a mechanic, also collected Coca-Cola antiques. When I first walked through Doug's house, I was struck with the way the house was littered—in no apparent order—with these relics of a faraway time. Trays and bottles and hubcaps and cartons and posters, all in the name of Coke. When I asked him why his father collected them, Doug's response was, "I don't know; he doesn't even drink the stuff." Also strewn throughout the house were beer cans, what his father apparently *did* drink.

Outside of passing nods from doorways and windows, I met Doug's parents only once. On Halloween night, my father's car idling in the driveway, I went to pick up Doug for trick-or-treating. Much to my surprise, Doug's father opened the door. He was a large man, with a crew cut exactly like his son's. His face was as disheveled and time-worn as his Coke art, and he had piercing eyes. Doug's mom was standing behind him, her appearance careful—hair and clothes tight to her body, as if she couldn't afford to let herself go. Even though she spoke with precision and confidence, her words seemed remarkably limp, almost defeated before they left her mouth. "Doug is coming down in a little bit," she said. "He decided to go as a ghost." I waited in strange silence.

Soon summer lapsed into fall and fall crept toward winter. For a week, Doug, my best friend for eight months running now, was in the Christmas spirit. He almost lived at my house, helping me bring in the freshly cut Christmas tree, the smell of evergreen on his hands. He helped decorate the tree too, bathed in the reflection of fire and the laughter of family. He laughed at the fat, rainbow lights, as if their bright, primary colors took him by surprise in such a gray, winter month.

We made angels in a hushed snow. We ate pumpkin pie by the fire. We played games like Crazy Eights, and listened to Johnny Mathis sing Christmas songs. Doug even stayed over one night, in a faded sleeping bag, and we giggled until 3 A.M. I showed him my mother's "secret" closet—the one where she hid all of the Christmas presents; I only peeked at one each year, I told him, otherwise it would shoot the whole season.

Doug slowed down for the first time since I had known him—in speech, in movement, in the blurring speed of his facades. He opened up to me. Once, while we walked in a heavy, windless snow at dusk, he told me his parents weren't much for Christmas. For them it consisted of a three-foot, plastic tree with tiny, antique Coke memorabilia, and a case of beer for Christmas Eve. His daddy, he said, usually immersed himself in his own version of the Christmas spirit. Her husband drunk, his mom would do the laundry and cry. "We're too poor, woman," his daddy would yell at her. "Just too poor."

Doug also told me that he liked my family: my dad, who wore his stupid Russian hat and whistled "O Holy Night" without knowing it; my mom, who always had warm hands and whose laugh rang with wild freedom. He would have never said what was deep in his heart— that this was as close to Christmas he had ever come— but you could see it in his eyes.

Doug and I talked about what we would do on Christmas Day. I was certain I was going to get a telescope for Christmas. "We'll climb up in the tree house and look at the moon and the stars," I promised him. Doug fell in love with the idea. He wanted to see if he could find another planet.

In the meantime, he continued to come to our house as much as he could. Once, as we were flying paper airplanes over snowmen candles, his plane landed on the tiny manger scene on the fireplace mantle; in fact, it nearly knocked Jesus clean out of his crib. I remember he asked me, quite out of the blue, if I believed in God.

I was a new Christian, still quite shaken by the idea of the cross, and had yet to find a way to put Jesus into words. I'm not sure the exact words I may have used, but the gist of it was, yes, I did believe in God. He smiled out of the corner of his mouth and said he'd like to believe too. Then, he picked up his plane from baby Jesus' lap and returned to his play.

There was always, in each of my childhood Christmases, the charge of anticipation. There was something in the smell of my father's Christmas fudge, in the cold of my ears after a shopping trip with my mother, in the sound of tape and scissors wrapping presents that made me feel as if something was breaking into reality that could never be put into words, something beyond all of the senses and whatever had once made sense. The biggest part of the joy of Christmas was the anticipation of getting there. And I was anticipating that this Christmas, with Doug, would be the best of all.

❧

For those of us who try to listen for the voice of God, we strain too often for what seems a distant whisper. The world, if it does anything well, blares with the drumming of power, the electric riffs of sex, the nervous clang of coins, the screams of self. It is not so much the level of the noise but the amount of dissonance, the hard-scrabbled places where endless questions repeat themselves.

It seems that we have been left to ourselves in a fearful and fallen world. Into each of our lives, there comes a time when we are no longer children—not just in the marking of years, but in a fundamental perspective about life. Somewhere along the line, the child-like qualities of trust, wonder, play, and imagination can no longer survive the crushing realities of adult life. Under the weight of the latest headlines, the responsibility of a new job, or the loss of someone or something dear to us, we lose what it means to believe like children. We lose pieces of ourselves, a little here, a little there, and pretty soon all of our attention is focused on the ever-present possibility of unraveling altogether. Only an adult can work this hard.

Having faith, which is all that is asked of us, is difficult when mothers fight their own children and tornadoes rip through towns; when fathers, for no apparent reason, lose their way, collecting long-forgotten realities to keep them from going to pieces.

Anyone knows that life is wild and random. As the Bible says, "He causes his sun to rise on the evil and the good, and sends rain on the rightous and the unrighteous" (Matthew 5:45). There is but one guarantee that the world offers—there are no guarantees.

Yet, in the midst of all this, there still survives a peculiar and most child-like hope. Of all the great surprises of the world, this is most certainly the greatest. Emily Dickinson writes:

Hope is the thing with feathers—
That perches in the soul—
And sings the tunes without the words—
And never stops—at all—

None of us, no matter how hard we might try, are immune to hope. Even the most strident atheist sees, in a flower, something unperishable. The most committed evolutionist, swimming in his own ooze, rises above the truth that seeks to drown him—the instinctual knowledge that there is a God. The most damaged heart, like a rusted wind chime, seeks again to sing in a summer breeze.

Lord Byron described hope as "Nothing but the paint on the face of Existence; the least touch of truth rubs it off, and then we see what a hollow-cheeked harlot we have got hold of." Cold facts would say as much. Yet, even in the ice of such reason, hope holds out, warms the heart. There has to be something more, something beyond or before or after this present human condition. Hope, writes one playwright, is the feeling you have that the feeling you have isn't permanent.

What of the hope of home? For those of us blessed by loving and free childhoods, there is in the word "home" a taste, a scent, a touch, like a garden strawberry, jasmine in May, or a breeze through a screen. For those broken or shattered as children, there is the hope of home as a healing balm, a coming in from the cold, a light in a distant window. For all of us, home is a seed of wild hope, the undeniable movement of the heart. Home is where we hope to journey and, even winded, what we see as still ahead of us.

We try, with all we can muster, to make it home. We love, but in our bruised need and wounded egos, hold back. We battle, but in the loss of blood, grow weary. We save and plug and patch, but in the mad leaking of the world, are always on the verge of being sucked under. We pray, but, more often than not, we prefer a safe rhythm to a dangerous God.

What is the hope of home for Doug, who, in the wildness of just one Christmas season, saw a tiny baby Jesus in a cradle and, always a step away from where he wished to be, wanted to believe in God? What is the hope of home for each of us? We are abandoned children, blinded both by evil and our own sin, walking in complete darkness with a flashlight—trying to find a way home, shins bleeding, toes stubbed, tongues tied, minds groping.

And, day after day after day, when all of our best efforts have failed, and home is still a distant and unreachable hope on the horizon, do we seek a short cut or an escape route or a bulldozer? Something to numb us or empower us or break through the pain?

Yet, still, no matter the exhaustion, the anger, the wounds received and inflicted, the dreams crashed and burning, we hope. And occasionally, when we come to an end of ourselves, we receive the unimaginable grace to believe, once again, like little children. We happen upon a field of fireflies deep into a July night, we hear the striking of a cathedral bell, the melody of voice on a Christmas eve, the grace-filled and impossible words of Luke as he writes:

> And there were shepherds living out in the fields nearby, keeping watch over their flocks at night. An angel of the Lord appeared to them, and the glory of the Lord shone around them, and they were terrified. But the angel said to them, "Do not be afraid. I bring you good news of great joy that will be for all the people. Today in the town of David a savior has been born to you; he is Christ the Lord. This will be a sign to you: You will find a baby wrapped in cloths and lying in a manger. (Luke: 2:8–12)

It takes a child, or one like a child to believe that on a Christmas day some two thousand years ago, in a horse stable, in the pungent scent of dung and hay, came the unexpected and unimagined breaking of redemption in the cry of a tiny baby. For unto you a savior has been born.

In Christ, the impossible became possible. Into time, eternity fell. The bloodshed of salvation came to wipe out the sin and violence and death. The joy of the cross came for a world wrapped in pain. Into the deadness of lives came the spirit of resurrection. Into old and weary hearts came a new creation. And, most unbelievable of all, this birthing of grace came not just once, but for every beating of a believing heart.

Into the groaning of creation, the Christmas story. In a stable, the eternal hope of home.

The last day I saw Doug, late into November, he was sad and quiet. As much as I tried to get him to play or talk, he withdrew even more. When my mother called us to supper, her words slipping over "Silent Night" on the stereo, Doug and I went to the bathroom to wash our hands. As he rolled up his sleeves, I saw bruises on his arms. I didn't think much about it at the time and probably would have never even given it a passing thought but for the teacher's announcement the next day at school. Doug and his parents had moved away. There was no explanation for the suddenness, only a faraway look on my teacher's face. I knew then that Doug, my best friend, had been beaten. Again.

On Christmas day that year, which I will forever mark as the end of my childhood, I remember opening my last gift—a telescope. Later, as night brought Christmas to a close, I climbed up into my tree house and looked at the moon and the stars. I knew, wherever he was, Doug was also staring into the sky, dreaming of faraway places. My best friend had gone before Christmas could ever come.

The Christmas story comes and goes, over and over and over, but if we are not careful how we look, we see nothing new in our lives. Life is filled with a more painful repetition. Year after year the story of Christmas yields to apparent reality.

The writer of Hebrews says, "In putting everything under him [Christ], God left nothing that is not subject to him. Yet at present we do not see everything subject to him" (Hebrews 2:8). Who could imagine, in two short sentences, such a swing of mood, such a bittersweet reality. Faith asks us to jump the yawning and violent gap between what has been accomplished and what will eventually be.

The 6 P.M. news tells us, in precise diction, of rapes, murders, child kidnappings, mail bombs, wars and rumors of wars, earthquakes, holes in the sky, holes in people, holes in hearts, holes in logic. In such an overwhelming cycle of pain and violence, most of us find that the best we can do is to reduce the size of our hearts to the amount of terror we can stand. We become safe, build walls and fences, watch sitcoms, and try to block out the whole stinking mess. But still it continues— children screaming and fighting, long hours at work, the slow-growing distance between husband and wife, mother and son, friend and friend.

For those with faith, if any remain, there is the nagging feeling that faith doesn't make much of a difference in the condition of a heart, and certainly not in the condition of a world going to pieces around us. The repetition seems to always move in the direction of breakage, decay, and apathy. Power or sex or violence are the only things that seem to get anyone by, and then only for a little while.

And yet we hope. Such a ridiculous hope. We long for things to be set right. We long for justice—for the powerful to be tried, sentenced, and punished for their exploitation of the weak. We long for lives filled with purpose, energy, and laughter. We long, like a child wrapped in the loving arms of a father, to be safe, valued, cherished. We long for home.

We long, most times without knowing it, for the Father in heaven. Romans 8:14–25 tells the bittersweet story of the journey of faith:

> Now if we are children, then we are heirs—heirs of God and co-heirs with Christ, if indeed we share in his sufferings in order that we may also share in his glory. I consider that our present sufferings are not worth comparing with the glory that will be revealed in us. The creation waits in eager expectation for the sons of God to be revealed.

Jesus said that if he went away, which he certainly did, he would be busy preparing mansions filled with love, beauty, light, and goodness for each one of us who has faith. We long to go home—where everything is right, and daughters don't do drugs, and cars don't break down, and husbands don't commit adultery, and little boys don't die of cancer, and the holy and righteous and loving Father wraps his arms around all of his precious and dear children and says, "Well done."

In the meantime, we groan and we hope.

> We know that the whole creation has been groaning as in the pains of childbirth right up to the present time. Not only so, but we ourselves, who have the firstfruits of the Spirit, groan inwardly as we wait eagerly for our adoption as sons, the redemption of our bodies. For in this hope we were saved. But hope that is seen is no hope at all. Who hopes for what he already has? But if we wait for what we do not yet have, we wait for it patiently. (Romans 8:23–25)

We groan in the incessant and tiring battle with sin, which tells us to give up hope and kick our own path to heaven. We groan for the Dougs of the world, children abandoned to violence, tasting here and there of home, wondering if faith can reach them. We groan with the Spirit, praying in language beyond words for redemption.

And, often just when we think we are beyond it, we hope. We hope for the unexpected and transforming power of the Christmas story, not just on December twenty-fifth, but in the mundane and sprawling days of the rest of our lives. We hope that the Spirit, like the sprouting of a tiny seed, can bring about the greening of new life. We hope for the perfect love of the Father in a perfect and sinless world.

And in both the groaning and the hope, when grace touches us, we are like little children on Christmas Day—wide-eyed, filled with wonder, open to possibility, imagining the best gift of all. In the waiting, we are transformed and moved by the permanence of the news that "Today in the town of David a savior has been born to you; he is Christ the Lord."

The beauty of a dandelion in seed, a voice on the wind, the Word of God rooted in your heart, the joyful dance of discipline, the wideness of God's love, the shadow of the cross: We experience all of these in the here and now, in the repetition of sin and evil and sparks of man, with a great, burning hope of heaven in the now and forever. Grace is this: the undeniable moment-by-moment birthing of a new creation for a child on his or her way home.